S0-FQK-749

TAKE UP YOUR
LIFE

TAKE UP YOUR LIFE

Making Spirituality Work
in the Real World

Janet Cedar Spring

Charles E. Tuttle Co., Inc.
Boston • Rutland, Vermont • Tokyo

First published in 1996 by Charles E. Tuttle Co., Inc.
of Rutland, Vermont, and Tokyo, Japan, with editorial offices at
153 Milk Street, Boston, Massachusetts, 02109

Copyright © 1996 Janet Cedar Spring

All rights reserved. No part of this publication may be reproduced or utilized in any form or by any means, electronic or mechanical, including photocopying, recording, or by any information storage and retrieval system, without prior written permission from Charles E. Tuttle Co., Inc.

The translation of *The Hsin Hsin Ming* that appears in the Appendix is copyright © 1996 Steve Hagen and is reproduced by permission.

Library of Congress Cataloging-in-Publication Data

Spring, Janet Cedar, 1948–
    Take up your life : making spirituality work in the real world / by Janet Cedar Spring.
       p. cm.
    Includes bibliographical references.
    ISBN 0-8048-3091-6
    1. Spirituality. 2. Spiritual life. I. Title.
BL624.S697 1996
291.4'4—dc20   96–10630
                                                          CIP

First edition

1 3 5 7 9 10 8 6 4 2   05 04 03 02 01 00 99 98 97 96

Cover and book design by Kathryn Sky-Peck
Printed in the United States of America

Contents

INTRODUCTION xi

1. The Dream Time 1
   Community and Ancient Memory 3
   Separation 9
   Take Down the Dulcimer 12
   Prepare a World for Our Children 15
   Invitation: Imagine 17

2. Life Is Like This 19
   Suffering 21
   Addiction and Escape 24
   The Point of No Return 28
   Virtue 30
   Invitation: Why? 33

3. We Want to Be Happy 35
   Taking Up a Practice 37
   Change or Die 39
   Grief 42
   Forgiveness 44
   Coming Home to Life 48
   Invitation: Release 52
         Transformation 53
         Presence 54

4. When You're the Other 55
- The Ugly Duckling 57
- Heyoka 62
- Silence 65
- Keep Your Own Mind 70
- Invitation: Read! 71
    - Grief Ritual 72

5. The Human Condition 75
- Darkness 77
- Shame 79
- Six States 82
- The Three Poisons 93
- Invitation: Exploring Anger 94
    - Embracing Forgiveness 96

6. Hope 99
- Beyond Suicide 101
- Going On 103
- So What? 107
- Breaking Open 109
- We Are Not Alone 111
- Invitation: Becoming the Holy 113

7. What Do You Do? 117
- Sit Down 119
- Just Stand Up 122
- Wrestle with God 123
- Practice 126
- Want 130
- Ask the Question 132
- Ask for Help 134

Enter the Maze 136
  Duty 137
  A Great Work 140
  Invitation: Following the Inner Guide 144

8. The Taste of Freedom 147
  What Cannot Be Named 149
  Give Thanks 151
  Birth and Death 153
  The Voice of Recognition 156
  Right There 158
  What Do You Do? 160
  Invitation: Gratitude: Part I 162
         Gratitude: Part II 163

Postlude 167

Appendix: *The Hsin Hsin Ming* 169
Notes 175
Author's Note 179
Some Favorite Books 183

Take Up Your
Life

Introduction

As long as you believe there is an easy answer, you cannot begin.

When you have tried and tried to ease your own suffering, and when you have failed and failed again, *then* you begin.

And somewhere deep in that beginning is hope, and the place where joy is born. There something starts to make sense.

I wrote this book because I know I am not alone. For perhaps thirty-five years (of my forty-six) I thought I was the only one who asked questions about the meaning of life, the only one who recognized the sacredness in every dance of falling leaf or snowflake, in the sun on the water or the wind in the cherry tree.

Finally I discovered there were others—not only long-dead poets and philosophers, but living human beings—who shared my search and my wonder. And slowly, gradually, I discovered that there are many more like me than I had ever hoped.

So I write, first, to pass along this fact: you are not alone. I write, second, to share my thoughts and provoke yours, and third, to offer tools that I hope will be helpful.

This book is for everyone who lives in the spaces between one religion and another, or between one religion and the vastness of empty space. It is for anyone who feels entirely lost, without even a place to set a foot. It is for those who are ardently spiritual but who lack a location, a community, a tradition, or a language. It is for those who are looking, but who do not even know how they will recognize what they seek if it appears before them. It is for those for whom spiritual homesickness is the defining fact of their lives.

I write not because I have exactly found home, but because I know the search so well. And because in my own search I have learned something about how to live on the road.

1

The Dream Time

> *Asked what is the most important question in life, Albert Einstein replied: "Is the universe a friendly place or not?"*

Community and Ancient Memory

We talk about community. Incessantly, obsessively, those of us who feel the alienation of modern life are talking and writing about community, about tribe, about how to make it happen or why it isn't working. We *know* something is missing, but we don't know what it is or how to get it.

When I look back at my childhood with an objective eye, it looks like that dream. My family had an acre of land, neighbors who stayed the same for ten years, and unlocked doors. I had a bicycle, woods and fields and freedom to roam. They told us children not to take rides from strangers, but I truly couldn't imagine why. I didn't carry a house key, or lock my bicycle, through the end of high school. The house was open, the bicycle safe.

I didn't notice it then. But later I noticed. First, it was when I couldn't give my own children the freedom I'd known. Later, when I listened to African American men tell stories of police harassment, when I knew too many women who'd been raped, when I watched the world around me and compared, then I noticed. Eventually I learned that I'd grown up in an idyllic, dreamlike setting.

In that protected childhood I listened sometimes to my parents talking about the way things used to be. The world was going downhill, it seemed, though I didn't know why. Some time in the past, things had been different. What I didn't know then was that they were doing their best to create for me that other time. Together with many other middle-class white Americans in the 1950s, they held the line against chaos and the modern age.

The "memory" of another time is common to most of us. We tend to imagine there was once a time—whether it was before the Industrial Revolution or before patriarchy, once upon a time or "when I was a kid"—when people loved and cared for each other, when life was simple and whole. In some deep place we are sure that there was a time when life was lived differently—when life *worked* for people like us. We "remember" that children were not afraid on the streets, that everyone watched and taught them, that elders were both respected and wise. We "remember" that at one time religion made sense, did not sound like empty words crying hopelessly in the face of the wind.

There is a book, called *The Way We Never Were*, that addresses this myth and takes it to pieces in terms of historical fact.[1] No, a hundred years ago American society was not kinder and gentler. And the opposite myth—that things are getting better and better—is addressed as well. Violence, discrimination, and poverty have not disappeared. Neither then nor now was the Golden Age, and it is doubtful we are progressing rapidly toward it.

Still, we set our sights and aim for it. We know how things ought to be.

For those of us who disbelieve the myth as memory, there is the dream: that someday we will live in peace. Imagine: to leave the apartment door unlocked; to walk, young, female, and pretty, unafraid down a city street alone at night; to walk, young, male, and large, unafraid in a neighborhood belonging to another race. Imagine being able to catch a ride, or pick up a stranger, without fear.

Imagine knowing that if someone asks for money or help she or he truly needs it; that you yourself can ask for help without being judged lazy and irresponsible. Imagine the abortion debate has simply disappeared because the need for it has become so rare—and the habit of judging each other has vanished. Imagine that you know most of your neighbors and are at home with them. Imagine that the "adopt-a-highway" teams plant flowers because there is no litter. Imagine life as whole, community as real. This is the dream.

There have indeed been times when life was much simpler, the individual's world much smaller. The tribe—twenty, a hundred, or five hundred people—was the primary space of existence; most people knew most of their neighbors most of their lives; a wanderer was an exception, a hero or deviant; a newcomer was still a newcomer twenty years later.

I lived in such a culture for a short time and fell in love with it. There was a warmth and friendliness that I still miss. I was greeted by strangers as I walked down the street; we looked one another in the eye; I felt *seen,* and welcome. I miss too the faces and body language of small children carried on their parents' backs, running everywhere unafraid, playing in puddles or on snow piles. Watching those children, I thought that their culture loves and wants children in a way that my own does not. That place has become for me in some ways the holder of this ancient memory.

And yet the dream can be a nightmare. The community that raised me was unable or unwilling to honor my emotional needs as a "different" child, so that my primary childhood memories center on humiliating episodes, repeated rejections, and the solace I found in the woods. In that other community I once saw a child literally evicted from home and village after accusing a respected citizen of sexually abusing her; she threatened their image of their community.

There was a fragility in both of these places. The responsible adults were fighting to maintain something valued against a change they feared. And their fears were reasonable, not fantasies. But their fear pushed them into denial, and they abandoned their own children. Thus they lost exactly the thing they were fighting to keep.

Forty years later I can see what my parents feared and agree they were right to fear. Still, the community they defended was not a good place for me—and denial is never an adequate protection anyway. Must community always be maintained by sacrifice, by scapegoating? I wish to believe not.

I choose to believe we can do better. This is my version of the dream: that we can have intact communities in which every person, *every* person, has a place.

We need the dream of community; we rely on it. It gives meaning to our struggles with modern life; it tells us where we are going. If people lack even a wish for a culture that would support and heal them, are they not missing a piece of humanity? Because we are not human alone; we are human only together. Even the hermit exists in relation to the community from which she lives apart. Tribe, village, community, all are part of our deepest definition.

Sometimes, living in vast cities and connected electronically with people across the world, we forget this. Told that several billion people are our own kind, we try to grasp it, and fail. We resent those who insist on holding that dream before us, or we judge those who give it up. We become alienated from those who once were our kinfolk as well as those we never knew or understood. We look for a small cluster of our own kind, whether what we share is racial, cultural, or ideological. It seems easier to make community with such an enclave, easier to shut out those who are different.

"Hate is not a family value," says the bumper sticker. Yet hate is intensely human. It comes from fear: fear that our own small cluster will be lost, that our family will be invaded, that the basic rules of living will be denied. This hate comes from the wish to protect what we perceive to be our own, to return to the exclusive, insulated community that seems possible when the new dream does not. This hate arises from the fear of losing something essential.

The ways of life that any of us have had in the past or have at present contain essential elements that teach parents how to raise children, elders how to make the transition to death, youth how to grow up, and all of us how to work together and how to meet the Infinite. These ways are precious, they are human, and they are imperfect. And they are not all the same.

The ancient memory of connection comes from a time long ago, when most of the people we saw were like us. To meet the dream, to make community with diversity, we must go through and beyond what our ancestors knew. A new way is called for: a way to keep our selves intact and also to open to otherness.

I do not know many languages, but I have noticed this: in many, many tongues, the word for "human" is the word for the tribe, and other tribes are called something else. Groups that have turned to hate are doing what humans have always done: they define a human race small enough for their own imagination, and name all others as enemy.

But the dream is true. We are one. Love is true, hate false; hope true, despair false. Community is real, alienation a lie. We are connected; we are one; we are whole.

Separation

In sixth grade in Lutheran parochial school, I was assigned to do a report on a church other than my own. I chose the Big One: the Roman Catholic Church. Following my own Lutheran training, I chose to study Catholicism by reading its catechism. In the public library I found a copy of the *Baltimore Catechism,* a standard text representing Catholic teaching. There I found a fascinating concept:

"What is sin?

"Sin is separation from God."

Sometime later in my life, I thought about the truism "No man is an island," and I felt its wrongness with my whole being. An island is attached to the whole earth. It only appears to be separate and isolated. What is a more apt description of our human state, our deluded state, the state of sin? We appear separate, we experience ourselves as separate, we are born and die separately. That word "sin," that terror, merely describes the human condition. This fundamental illusion, that we are separate from each other, is the cause of all suffering.

Shunryu Suzuki, Roshi, a modern Zen master, said that "To look at a flower and say 'That is beautiful' is sin."[2] At first this seemed to me a strange, uncomfortable thought. But eventually I understood.

When you look at an object and judge it—whether you

decide it is good or bad, beautiful or ugly—you are separating yourself from it. You are imagining yourself as solo; you are going off on your own. You are cutting off your interconnection with all beings, your absolute connection with God, who is in—who is—all beings and all things. This cutting off is itself original sin, understood in Christianity as the condition of all human beings—a condition we cannot escape.

To be born human, to enter this world with mind and consciousness, is to enter the experience of separateness. Thus we all, by definition, are in a state of sin. To refuse this state is to refuse to be human, to refuse to join our companions in the great journey. It is to refuse to be of any use to anyone but ourselves.

To become human, to enter a realm in which suffering, wanting, anger, and disappointment abound, is to join other beings in the great way of liberation. To allow ourselves to be hurt and to recognize our own pain in the pain of others is to support all beings in becoming free from suffering.

To willingly enter a state of sin is a great gift. Some people have entered it so fully that they never catch a glimpse beyond the delusion. The rest of us, half-awake, may learn from their suffering.

We are able to recognize and honor those beings who come to us with clear consciousness and teach.

I was taught as a child that Jesus was both human and god. We knew he experienced physical pain, but we weren't so sure that he felt emotional pain. Yet, in the clear awareness of his last hours, as he cried, "My God, why have you forsaken me?"[3] he suffered. He came all the way into human suffering, into separation, even into sin.

Buddha, it is said, was born an ordinary human, focused his attention on the problem of suffering, and woke up. He stayed in life, in suffering, in the experience of sin for the purpose of helping others to wake up too.

All awakened ones come into the world for the purpose of teaching, helping, communicating with other beings—indeed, with *all* beings. Their essential nature is connection, oneness. And yet, if we insist on staying only in this oneness, if we refuse to enter the illusion of separation, we cannot talk to each other. We are then profoundly separated. Refusing to sin, we sin.

All of this appears as part of the dream time, part of the pervasive myth of a time and place (Once upon a time; someday) where humans were (will be) connected, as a matter of course, with each other, with other beings, and with the entire world. We will all belong; we will all have our rightful place.

The dream is both part of the truth, reminding us that connection is our natural state, and part of the illusion, suggesting that connection happens somewhere other than here and now. This myth, the dream, lies within, behind, and beneath every moment and every interaction—from the welcoming home of a beloved friend to an act of violence committed by a stranger in the street. It is there: But how do we wake up to it?

Take Down the Dulcimer

We wake up every morning empty and frightened. Don't go to the study and begin reading. Take down the dulcimer. Let the beauty that we love be what we do. There are a hundred ways to kneel and kiss the ground.

—RUMI, *OPEN SECRET*

Under a wide starry sky, I hear screams and have to decide whether to dial 911, take some more direct action, or explain the screams away.

On a city sidewalk, children play amid broken glass and throw candy wrappers to blow among the lilacs.

In a quiet rural township, the Jefferson Town Hall stands boarded up and unmarked beside a winding road. "Every time we put up the sign, they shoot it full of holes," says the town clerk.

On the radio, each day brings a hundred reminders that on the scale of human suffering, complaints such as these are trivial indeed.

Thus the world interrupts our search for peace.

If our quiet place cannot coexist with the suffering of ordinary life, it is only escape and not freedom.

❦

I watch the interplay between forces: the police and the gangs, the Far Right and the Far Left and their more moderate counterparts, rigid violence and chaotic violence. On both sides are human beings who believe themselves right; on both sides they imagine the other as hateful, uncaring, dangerous, perhaps a little less than human. Thus each loses a little more of its humanity.

Where are the forces that are actually human and humane? Where is healing, where hope? Where does compassion guide decisions and wisdom inform them?

Gradually a list forms in my mind—a list of people who work for justice without causing dissension, people who seek peace without forgetting truth, organizations dedicated to freedom that also remember community. None are perfect; what matters is that they are there at all.

My list will not be yours. Look at the people you know and make your own list. If you cannot, here is a source: go to your daily mail and take up the solicitations for funds by organizations that somehow got your name. Open your heart and read them. Consider whether any of these people are cause for hope in humankind.

❦

Let there be something in life besides serious study, worry, and political struggle. And let there be something in life besides earnest spiritual work, the effort toward enlightenment. Also let there be something besides taking care of one's own life and family, besides a good living and a good retirement, besides vacations and pleasures.

Let there be a life that is full and connected. Let there be play, dance, music, and laughter. In the face of terrible knowledge, let there be laughter. Let loving and lovemaking abound even in the presence of death. As the cycle of seasons stops for no one, so let the rhythms of human life never quit.

And so it is right to make a work of art, to conceive a child, to pursue an invention for its own joy, to build a home, to seek enlightenment, to cook a fine meal. All these are in harmony with the rhythms of life.

It is *not* right to let any of these things become the whole of existence. For then you are no longer part of humanity. You belong only to your own club, to the people who share your particular venture, and not to the whole.

When I say "right," I mean this: there is a sense, a place, a moment when everything belongs, when things move harmoniously together, when you can feel that everything is exactly as it ought to be. This moment might well be called truth, or beauty, or enlightenment; or it can be called right, proper, or in sync. In such moments, the dream time breaks through the veil and appears in ordinary reality.

Prepare a World for Our Children

People talk about preparing our children for the world. I would rather prepare a world for my children.

—UNKNOWN

We each need an opening to others. We open to our friends, to our family, to lovers and life partners, in one way. We open to coworkers and neighbors in another way. In yet another we open to people we have never met.

If we close off any of these ways, we are not connected, not in harmony, not in sync. Our own natural rhythms are cut off, as are the relationships around us, distorted by the ways we have removed ourselves.

To be human is to be connected, and also at times to be disconnected. We dare not expect ourselves to stay open at all times to all people, yet we must not expect less—and *this* is what it means to live in illusion (in sin). This is what it means to be an island.

We know essentially and instinctively the difference between right and wrong, between connection and disconnection. The most important thing we can do is forgive ourselves, forgive each other, repent and return to each other again and again and again. We can talk endlessly of national issues, but where we make a difference is here in our own homes, relationships, families, and workplaces. Here, today, we return to each other and return to harmony.

We do it individually, and we do it together. We meet each other, even from a very great distance; we make space for each other in spite of how little we have for ourselves. We learn to move in rhythm with others, even with those whose rhythm seems to us impossible, and even when our own rhythm seems hopelessly lost.

Thus we can prepare a world for our children and the generations to follow.

We can prepare a world where our children and grandchildren can be as young as they actually are, because they do not have to learn unpleasant lessons too early. A world where human beings will live, not only exist. A world in which fear and its limitations, hate and its barriers, are only small parts of what shapes daily existence.

We can prepare a world in which each child has some real experience of trust, both given and honored, so the next generation will know what trust feels like.

A child who has been able to believe her elders will have the ability someday to believe herself. A child whose world is based on reliable adults will grow into an adult able to act with certainty. A child who has been trusted—as a child, not as an imitation adult—will develop a knowing deep in his body that makes possible a life based on truth.

Such children grow into adults for whom decisions naturally come from a place of connection rather than a place of fear. Such children grow into adults who will be able to build the next world.

Thinking that we can't do it all in my generation, maybe not in my lifetime, I weep. Thinking that the healing may ever happen, that some day humans may live in peace, I weep again. The first tears are the price for the second.

Invitation

Imagine

Imagine, the next time someone does you harm, that the person came into this world for the express purpose of freeing you from suffering. Imagine that the cruelty or thoughtlessness is part of a larger design to help you wake up.

Imagine, the next time you are impatient with someone's ignorance, clumsiness, or stubbornness, that you came into this world for the express purpose of freeing that person from suffering. Imagine that the behavior is a cry for help, asking you to be awake enough to hear and respond, asking your compassion to move in a way that supports the person's liberation from ignorance, clumsiness, or stubbornness.

2

Life Is Like This

> A woman came to the Buddha carrying her infant son, who had died. She wanted him to make her son alive again.
>
> The Buddha listened, then said, "All right, I will do that if you will bring me three mustard seeds." The woman was overjoyed.
>
> The Buddha continued, "But those seeds must each come from a house that has not known death."
>
> She set out looking. She went from house to house asking for a mustard seed and then inquiring whether anyone had died there.
>
> Nowhere was there a house without death.
>
> Finally she returned to the Buddha and said, "Show me something more enduring than life."
>
> —TRADITIONAL BUDDHIST STORY

Suffering

Pain is the experience; suffering is the story we tell ourselves about what we experience.
—LAR SHORT,
LECTURE IN MINNEAPOLIS, MAY 25, 1993

The word "suffering" is the most common English translation for the Sanskrit word *"dukkha,"* whose basic meaning is something like "unsatisfactoriness." In Sanskrit *"dukkha"* evokes an image of a wheel out of true. Every time it goes around, *bump!*—discomfort and noise.

The second definition of "suffering" comes from the English root meaning itself: "to bear up under." The image we have is of someone carrying a heavy weight—but not being crushed or stopped by it. Another meaning is "to allow."

With physical pain, we come right up against powerlessness. With a broken arm, we may be able to reduce the painful stimuli to the brain through medications or visualizations, but there's no question about the arm being broken. There are things we can do ourselves (apply ice, stay immobile, take medication), things we can get help for (setting the bone), and things we must wait for the body to do (mend the tissues). Prayers or alternative healing may speed the mending, but the process still needs to happen. There may or may not be emotional suffering, but there is real, straightforward physical pain.

With emotional pain, the balance is on the story we tell ourselves that makes us hurt. It is always a story of real or potential loss—a relationship ended, a loved one died, a blow to our self-esteem—and we feel pain.

We could say it is our attachment to what we are losing that causes the pain. In a sense this is true, but it is also incomplete. The pain of loss is the pain of choosing to be human. The only way to escape this pain is to deny our humanness by refusing to love. However much we may talk of loving and letting go, to love as humans love is also to want, to enjoy, to wish for the presence of the loved one. Desire is part of being human, and its natural consequences are sadness and loss. Enlightenment does not end this any more than enlightenment ends the straightforward pain of the broken arm.

Yet, whether our pain is emotional or physical, we *can* eventually let go, we can end the story, we can have just the pain and not the enormous suffering of "I don't want this" or "Why did this happen to me?"

Physical pain comes and goes, and all we can do is allow it to come and go. Sometimes we can partly control it; often we cannot.

Shunryu Suzuki, Roshi, said that to renounce attachment simply means to accept that things come and go.[4] But then what? Accept that a pain-free body also comes and goes? That you will be intermittently swept with pain so intense that even to breathe requires conscious effort? That the pains will come and will not leave, that there will be no medical explanation, and eventually that the painkillers will cease being effective?

Yes, if that is what life brings you.

~

Physical pain is where we really learn, if we are able, to let go of attachment.

In one part of my work, I interact with human bodies and minds using an approach known for releasing pain and ending suffering. My experience is that much suffering is unnecessary, that it can be relieved—by positioning or moving the body in certain subtle but simple ways, by emotional release, or by both of these things in combination with energy interaction and ongoing exercises. More pain can be relieved than most people imagine.

Yet the fact that I usually am able to help makes it more difficult when I meet pain that I *cannot* help. When people in severe pain finally are forced to acknowledge that the pain cannot be helped, they then must find a way to accept the utterly unacceptable. Watching their tears, and sometimes their despair, I ask myself, "Is all this necessary before their next opening can begin?"

I dare not stand behind such people and tell them that they are on their way to higher consciousness. All I can do is be with them in compassion, and rejoice if I see release and movement. As indeed I rejoice if the pain itself drops away.

Pain is real. Life contains suffering. This is the first great truth of Buddhism.

Addiction and Escape

Hobbes: Whatcha doin'?
Calvin: Getting rich!
Hobbes: Really?
Calvin: Yep. I'm writing a self-help book! There's a huge market for this stuff. First, you convince people there's something wrong with them. That's easy because advertising has already conditioned people to feel insecure about their weight, looks, social status, sex appeal, and so on. Next, you convince them that the problem is not their fault and that they're victims of larger forces. That's easy, because it's what people believe anyway. Nobody wants to be responsible for his own situation. Finally, you convince them that with your expert advice and encouragement, they can conquer their problem and be happy!
Hobbes: Ingenious. What problem will you help people solve?
Calvin: Their addiction to self-help books! My book is called Shut Up and Stop Whining: How to Do Something with Your Life Besides Think About Yourself.
Hobbes: You should probably wait for the advance before you buy anything.
Calvin: The trouble is . . . if my program works, I won't be able to write a sequel.
—From the "Calvin and Hobbes" comic strip
by Bill Watterson [5]

If the measure of our suffering can be seen in the effort we make to end it, humankind is hurting enormously. And the largest part of that hurt is emotional.

Take Up Your Life

Famine, war, and torture are present daily in our lives, not because most of us experience them personally, but because they are brought to us by television, radio, and the press. The news media make it their business to make these things real, to make us understand that it's human beings like us who are being starved, raped, and tortured—and who are doing the starving, raping, and torturing. And we can do precious little about it. So we criticize our leaders, pretending that, if they were wiser or better, they would be able to stop it all.

A few of us, a very few, are able to ease our own helplessness by volunteering to work in places of calamity. They choose the suffering of more fully knowing the intensity of the suffering, in exchange for being able to do something to help. Letting in the flood of anguish, they buy a little peace.

As for the rest of us—those who are not busy with physical or economic survival, or with trying to raise healthy children in the midst of a war or drug zone—we cope with the sheer immensity of the pain by closing our eyes, by distancing ourselves, by shutting it out.

There are lots of ways of doing this.

1. Get very busy with the details of your life. Work hard.

2. Alcohol, drugs, chocolate, and food can provide temporary relief. Organizing your life around them can become a long-term distraction from the pain; the added suffering they cause in and of themselves will finish the job.

3. Sex, gambling, and romance can work about the same way.

4. Try self-perfection—in athletics, appearance, emotional health, work, parenting, spirituality. Focus all your energy on producing yourself as a work of art.

5. Take up a cause, get into politics, get into righteous anger, and work at fixing the root of the problem, based on:

6. Analyzing, explaining, intellectualizing, anything that will make this look like a solvable problem rather than a permanent condition.

7. If all these fail, move into hopelessness, revenge, vandalism, or violence at any level, small or large, subtle or overt. Become part of the problem. Hate.

8. When you get tired of all of these, join a cult, religious or otherwise, that offers simple answers and encourages you to turn your back on other humans and ordinary life, in exchange for a life of bliss with your guru or leader.

All of these are ways that we try to control pain—by denying that it exists, by looking the other way, or by pinning it down and dissecting it. All are described here in their extreme forms, but their subtle forms are hard for anyone to avoid. We all do them to some extent, and we are so accustomed to them that, for the most part, we don't notice.

Distancing is a way of medicating our emotional pain. By holding ourselves back from suffering thus, we weaken ourselves, and become less and less able to cope with new situations. As we become numb to pain, we also lose touch with the life force, with our power to do anything about the pain. Protecting ourselves from violence, we do subtle violence to ourselves and each other.

We have come about as far as we can in this direction; soon, in order to survive as a people, we must find new ways of facing both pain and helplessness.

The Point of No Return

There is an African people called the Ik. For centuries the Ik lived in a region of abundance and had a happy and generous culture.

At some point, however, their hunting area was taken over as a game refuge, forcing them to become farmers in a desert. Over the years they adapted their customs to deal with their newfound scarcity. Tradition still demanded that if visitors came while you were eating, you had to invite them to eat with you. However, the impact of poverty on this custom was that whenever people got food, they would hide to eat it alone.

The entire Ik culture unraveled. People threw their children out of their homes at the age of three and stole food from their aging parents. An old woman fell down and no one helped her up; she would have died quickly, except for the visiting anthropologist, who could not bear it. He wrote later that he regretted his action: she'd been laughing with the others at how funny she looked, but then remembered the kindness her people had lost and died in sadness.

The Ik finally came upon good times again. Rain fell, and food was abundant. But they had forgotten how to live with abundance. They ate freely, but the extra food rotted on the vine instead of being stored in the old ways.

The Ik were destroyed by too much hardship.[6]

It seems as though there is a point of no return. It seems as though a community can get to a place where all that can be done is to finish dying. Even if some miracle happened, the best such a community could do would be to die with grace. I would not want to say this is true, but it seems so.

Consider the impact of severe alcoholism on a culture. Children born with fetal alcohol syndrome—the result of their mothers' heavy drinking during pregnancy—are unable to learn, to think for the future, to distinguish between friend and stranger, to make ordinary human relationships. They are very friendly, but they cannot bond; they can have sexual relations but cannot parent; they grow larger but not mature; and they may have to be watched throughout their entire lives for their own safety.

In this way, a people with an alcoholic culture can commit collective suicide in a few generations. In this way, a conquering society can commit genocide on the defeated without ever being blamed—simply by substituting intoxicants for spirituality, entertainment for real work, and possessions for integrity and self-respect.

Virtue

What we need is virtue: virtue in its original meaning, "strength." We need morality; we need charity; we may even need sacrifice.

All of these are words of religion. And, to one degree or another, all of them have come to be associated with weakness, with accepting authority instead of thinking for yourself, with doing what you're told instead of deciding for yourself what to do.

All religions point to something beyond, something larger than the individual human, whether that something is called God, Spirit, the universe, true nature, our ancestors, or whatever. All religions invite us to regard ourselves as relatively small and not all-powerful. This invitation can be experienced as either frightening and shaming ("I'm nobody," "I can't do it by myself") or as liberating ("I don't have to do it by myself.")

In addition, most religions (from charismatic Christianity to New Age prosperity consciousness to modern Wicca) include the possibility of miracles, either through actively seeking intervention by an outside being or by realigning yourself so that the natural laws of the universe benefit you.

If you are operating in the shame-and-fear mode, an unsuccessful attempt at a miracle (or a prayer not answered visibly or promptly enough) becomes a failure, evidence that your faith is too

Take Up Your Life

weak or your intention not clear. This can bring on self-reproach, self-defense, or an effort to clean up your act (often an effort to fix what was not broken). What *was* broken was the initial relationship with the whole, something these desperate efforts cannot repair.

The true function of religion is as a container for the water of life—the unknown, the Mystery—something that remembers us as part of the Great Mother, that experiences and reveals the boundlessness of the sky. This is usually called "spirituality" these days, a paltry word for the taste of immortality and the memory of heaven deep in our bones.

Religions have been rightly castigated for limiting the spirit, reducing it first to form and then further to a lifeless form. Yet a religion may be worn out and dying in its native land and simultaneously spirit-filled and alive in some new place. Or it may come alive while under attack or during times of great trial.

Lifeless or not, religion *is* form because it must hold something. You can't carry spirit without a form any more than you can carry water without a container. People who attempt to have spirituality without religion, then, have to metaphorically live next to the spring all the time in order to be able to drink.

Pure spirituality might include walking in the woods, sitting with a dying person, playing with a baby, or following one's breath. But as soon as the process is remembered as useful, passed on or shared, it has become religion: a form for carrying spirit, a finger pointing the way.

Religion is a human activity, an act of community, a way of bringing spirituality into the realm of real life.

An essential quality of religion is sacrifice. From the Latin "to make holy," sacrifice always means to make a choice. To sacrifice is to release the lesser in order to realize the greater. To invite in the sacred, we shut out some things; we draw a boundary, we state a preference, we create a form.

In daily routine, sacrifice may mean not answering the phone so we can stay fully focused during meditation or worship; or it may mean being willing to interrupt that same focus to answer the call of a genuine need. It can mean setting aside your own needs to care for your child, or saying a difficult "no" to your child's wants for the sake of something more essential. There is a way of making holy each moment, place, and situation.

Sacrifice often occurs in extraordinary events, up to and including the sacrifice of one's life for the sake of others. In all cases, the meaning is the release of the lesser in order to realize the greater—releasing personal gain (or even personal existence) to become the embodiment of love. Always, the result is something more valued than the thing sacrificed.

When the sacrifice is real, when the sacred has been found, when religion is a container for the living water of spirit, then virtue and morality abound, compassion and wisdom prevail. Then strength meets wisdom and is able to face suffering, even tragedy, without flinching. Then religion is alive and whole, bringing spirit into life as its nature requires. Then we are able to search for the dream in its largest sense, drawing the entire universe into ourselves, embracing the whole of life, becoming the dream itself.

This naturally fosters community. But it happens one human being at a time.

Invitation

Why?

Imagine that it is up to you to assign meaning to life, to explain why pain, suffering, cruelty, and violence exist in the world. What meaning would you give?

Now imagine that this exercise is real, that there actually is no objective reason for the difficulties in life. Does this cause you pain or relief? How so? Write or talk about it until you have at least some understanding of your response.

3

We Want to Be Happy

> "We are here," said the teacher, "because we want to be happy. We want not just a little happiness, but the great happiness. And we want it not just for a while, but for all time."
> —UNKNOWN

Taking Up a Practice

I have always known that at last I would take this road.
But yesterday I did not know
It would be today.

—NARIHARA, ELEVENTH-CENTURY JAPANESE POET

In 1983 I walked innocently into the Minnesota Zen Center, with no idea that my life would be changed by doing so.

I held out for three years there, not knowing why I was there and certain that I would never again take up a religion. I listened to the lectures and thought I understood them. I liked Zen philosophy.

In 1986 I sat down for a seven day meditation retreat. And then I began to understand that I did not understand at all, that this was nothing like philosophy. And the glass walls inside my heart began to shatter. The shards pierced me; I wept and was glad.

I spent hours weeping over my stupidity and stubbornness. I'd never thought I was asleep or numb, but now I found a vast living space open before me and within me that I'd never imagined existed.

Soon after this time, I discovered a saying: "Everything you encounter is your life." I typed this sentence on a small piece of paper and taped it to the inside of my desk drawer at work. When the pressures of the job (county social work) or the irritation of my work neighbors got to be too much, I would open my drawer, look at the quote, and consider that all these unreasonable situations were part of my life. What was I going to do about it—right now? It helped me to get through that job, one day at a time, until it was time to leave.

Suzuki Roshi told his disciples that spiritual practice is like a train; once you get on, you can't get off. Once you are on, the ride brings much suffering. And no desire causes as much suffering as the desire to end suffering. Yet once the journey is begun, this desire is impossible to abandon except at its completion.

When you take up a spiritual practice, you no longer avoid suffering. Instead you enter it fully, knowing that someday in this life or another you will be free of it.

Being free of suffering does not mean the end of pain; rather, it means being able to live with pain and not be taken over by it, not lose your mind because of it, not feel driven to escape through compulsions or addictions.

The spiritual path entails loneliness. Taking it up, you bear your own burdens fully and then welcome those of others. "Why me?" is replaced by "Why not me?"—and, ultimately, a willingness to receive the pain of others.

There is no point in running away from suffering, because it always follows us. We may as well turn and face it, meet it, embrace it; then we will have only the suffering and not the running. And running interferes with the joy that also is present in every moment.

Change or Die

I know only this: there is no how. There is only your intention, and mine, and as far as I know that settles it.

—EVANGELINE, FRIEND AND MENTOR

To face the wound, to face the pain, to admit just how difficult things are: this is the place to start.

We are all of us in some mixture of pain and joy, thinned with numbness until the pain is tolerable. The trouble is, the numbness stops the joy as well. And releasing it brings back the pain.

We look for but cannot find one place to lay the blame for life's irrationality. We see people seeking survival and then, when that seems assured, comfort. Then, by some kind of mistake, the accumulation of wealth becomes an end in itself. We see scarcity where none need exist, and the creation of endless so-called needs whose only function is to distract us from the numbness of ordinary existence.

Our healing begins with the wound itself.

When it gets too painful, you have to let go—go into the sorrow, the depth of pain, the agony of existence, the frank admission of your own foolishness.

And then you have to stand up.

You have to give up, forget you were a victim, forget how foolish you've been, forget about your own wound—or carry it with you as an advisor—and do what needs to be done.

Wars and natural disasters call forth this quality in people, this doing what needs to be done. In the ongoing emergency of modern life, this quality still comes forth, but less clearly and with less frequency. Yet more and more of us can see that we are in a corner, that it's time to change or die.

If anything will save us, it is this awareness.

We need compassion. We need it first for ourselves, then to spread to our families and to those around us. We need it to be like a fountain, like a spring flowing up from the ground where we all can drink, or like a well from which all can draw water.

We need to take one step forward, to simply do the next thing. Rest, eat, work, talk. Do the next thing.

Don't pretend it's not real. Don't pretend it's not happening. Admit what's going on. Admit that your heart is broken. Admit whatever it is.

Don't try to fix it or think there's an easy answer. Don't even try to interpret it in ways that make sense.

Don't try to escape. All those options for avoiding the pain—don't take them. They're death.

Be a grown-up. Think. Don't wait for someone else to fix it.

This is hard. Let it be hard.

Dainin Katagiri, Roshi, the Zen master who taught in

Minneapolis until his death in 1990, said that it's when you're in a corner that you can finally get out. When you're at the end of your rope, when all your options are exhausted, *then* you can get free.

Another modern-day Zen teacher, Teijo Munnich, says that the end of your rope comes only after suicide is no longer an option. After you've let go of all the tempting routes toward a fast death, or a living death through some form of escape, then you can reach the possibility of breaking through to freedom.

Compassion is pain-with, suffering-with. Somewhere in life, after all the alternatives are gone, something opens inside. Then the unbearable and the impossible find room inside your heart.

Grief

Grief seems to me like a winter house: guarded, sheltered against an outside world that's expected to be difficult. The windows are small to keep out the cold, and little light gets in. The darkness and warmth make a cozy place to hide, to nurse wounds, to incubate what is not yet ready to be exposed.

Because there is change, because life includes death, because not all hopes come to pass, grief will be present as long as life goes on. And yet, as part of life, grief too must end.

Grief comes, taking us by surprise, and leaves—sometimes as suddenly, sometimes not. Sometimes it is as difficult to let it go as it is to pack away the winter clothes when a May snowstorm is still a possibility. But to live permanently in grief is to avoid life.

Sometimes it seems as though we fear change even more than we fear loss and grief. How dare we open to joy, knowing that it will surely end? What is amazing is that we dare it at all.

To accept grief as a foundation, then, is to receive it, to allow that it will come and go, to accept that we may well be struck again when we least expect it.

If we cannot receive the coming and going of grief, we cannot enter the other side of life. If we would cherish the smile of a baby, the drift of cherry blossoms in springtime, the heart's leap responding to a lover's glance—if we would embrace the joys of life, we must receive their loss. Otherwise, defended, we miss the whole show.

To stand on grief as a foundation is to stand on something that moves. This is what is the hardest. When we first admit grief, it seems to mean that we must move into it as a permanent home. But it means something harder still: going on with the dance, knowing that at any moment we may be struck down once more.

We have learned to pretend that death does not happen unexpectedly. Yet anyone who has been surprised by cancer, or injured in a natural disaster, or hit by a car or a terrorist's bullet, knows differently. Seeking causes and explanations helps us imagine we can prevent the next time—but if the next time is a drunken driver on a bridge, we may die.

On this, because we are human, we can stand.

Forgiveness

Forgiveness is the wide open space that allows us to be human. It is a mother's arms receiving the child who has done something wrong and knows it. It is the space of returning home.

We do not know what will happen next in life, nor why it happens. We make up explanations—individually, as families, as nations, as religions, and as whole cultures. We want to *know* so we can predict, choose our course, attempt to control our lives at least a little bit. But the truth is that we do *not* know.

Sometimes it seems obvious that there is an orderly cause-and-effect pattern to life. At other times events make absolutely no sense to us. We try to make them orderly or comprehensible; we find comfort in relying on God's will or on the laws of karma, the Protestant ethic or the discoveries of science. Whatever our religion, we can turn its teachings into a protection against the uncertainties of life.

But there's another way. We can hold the same teachings softly, and walk forward into our lives just as they are. The way of forgiveness coexists with every teaching; it makes its own space without denying any of the others. Forgiveness makes it possible to release our tight hold on explanations and simply stand in the watery ground of not-knowing.

Everything changes, yes. Cause leads to effect, yes. Whatever arises, ceases. This too shall pass, whether sorrow or delight. This is forgiveness.

Nothing you have done is carved in stone, neither who you are nor what you want. You can change, and you may be changed. With every breath you die and are reborn. This, surely, is forgiveness.

Every seven years all the cells of your body have changed, and you are a new person. Nothing lasts. Why, then, cling to the past, to ancient sufferings and old woes? To be new each moment: *Why not?*

That question is real and calls for a serious answer. The answer lies in two directions. In one direction is our fear of what we do not know. In the other direction are the people in our lives and their expectations of us—to pay the rent, to show up at work, to come home each night, to continue to love them. To begin anew each moment would suggest forgetting not only our fears, not only our obligations, but also our loved ones. To stay human, then, we need the memory that carries these connections. Yet memory inevitably includes past injuries, mistakes, and sufferings—it is the breeding ground for fear and anger.

How, then, are we to be free of memory without losing it—how can we keep our history and humanness and still be reborn each moment? How can we be free of our mind without losing its wonderful abilities? How can we be fully conscious and individual, enter into promises, remember all of the past, experience ourselves as received and embraced by life, take the hard with the pleasant, the grief with the joy—and still enter fully into each day?

The beginning of such a life is the simple act of turning toward it.

This step is called repentance and is found in all religions. Repentance means to turn back, to come home, to accept the mother's embrace. Its central meaning is *not* in the harsh edge of "I did something wrong" but in "I am willing to receive, I am willing to come home, I am willing to be restored and forgiven."

Forgiveness keeps coming back to the beginning. Forgiveness is about merciful change; it is a moving, pulsing embrace of the ever-changing ocean of life. What is thrown away or cast out may refuse to leave or may return another time; in either case we must receive it, embrace it, forgive it.

Forgiveness ripples softly along the water, blows through the treetops. It moves in the skin, reaching out from one hand to another. It comes forth and rubs your shoulders when you are most tense, have made the worst mistakes. At such times forgiveness whispers, "You are still human."

Forgiveness *means* that you are still human, and there is nothing else you need to be. There is nowhere you need to go. You do not need to be anything but human, and the ebb and flow of life happens inside you as well as outside. Everything arises and ceases, arises and ceases, and you are still here; we are all still here.

We all call the same place home: true nature, self, God. It is the clear pure water of the spring; it is the bedrock below the ocean, on which the various islands stand. All of us remember this, return to this, reach our roots into it, and drink from its waters.

Forgiveness means it is all right to be human. But we, who are all broken, must offer that right to each other. We must make space for each other's brokenness and hardness, our cruelty and frailty. We must make space for each other in spite of how little we may have for ourselves.

Here forgiveness becomes a spiritual practice, a hard practice. It requires us to lower our barriers, to break down our walls, and sometimes to risk our own sense of our selves, in order to remain in relationship with another.

To offer that sweet connection, indeed to insist on it—this practice brings us back to the place where we *are* one, the source, the bubbling spring, the fountain of life.

Here we move out of the winter house and let its walls crumble; here we live on the open plain, whether the wind blows gently or fiercely; here the clear, pure water of the spring runs in our veins, and the breath of all beings moves in our lungs.

Coming Home to Life

The sweetness of forgiveness stands against and happens within the movement of grief, rising and falling, never knowing what will come next.

By our human nature, we seek what lasts. We build strong houses against winds and storms and earthquakes. Or we learn to live in tents, to build and rebuild temporary shelters, relying on our skill and flexibility rather than on our houses. We seek permanence, one way or another.

Yet to abandon permanence is to allow more room for the sweetness, the kiss, the morning dew, the call of the loon against the stillness of the evening lake. To abandon permanence, to embrace impermanence, is to invite the kiss of life. This is done by not avoiding pain, sorrow, or death.

And still there is more. Impermanence alone cannot sustain us; in the end we must abandon it as well.

So, then, to abandon impermanence is to be willing to stay, to allow commitment, to truly enter this life. It is to remain when things get hard in a relationship or a job or a community. It is to develop some muscle, some internal strength, some personal power, rather than to run away from difficulty.

To abandon impermanence is to take responsibility for how

life works, for how your life works, and for your contribution to your relationships and community. It means not to cling to being a wanderer.

Impermanence is real. Everything passes. Pain ends, though for some people it ends only with death. Pleasure also ends. Nothing lasts, neither pain nor pleasure, and so we must stand somewhere that is neither.

In Buddhism there is something called taking refuge. We take refuge in the Buddha, the *dharma,* the *sangha:* the awakened one, the teaching, and the community.

Buddha means "the awake" or "the good." It is the name given to a historical person and to a quality. To take refuge in Buddha means to take refuge in the fact that it is possible to be awake, to place our feet firmly on the ground of not-knowing, not-controlling. To give up hiding. To abandon protection.

This is stark and frightening sometimes, exhilarating sometimes, and often just boring. It is all there is.

It includes acknowledgment that being awake is possible and has been experienced before, and gratitude to those who have traveled the road before us and put up signposts.

Buddha is that home place, the place where we all are one. To take refuge in Buddha is to attempt to know ourselves as awake, to be willing to know it, to receive awakeness as a dwelling place and the only roof over our heads.

Thus monks are referred to as home-leavers: because they abandon every other home and make awakeness their only home. They do so even before they have found it.

A monk asked, "What is the most miserable state?" His teacher said, "The most miserable state is to have begun the monk's journey and not have resolved the Great Matter."[7] That is, to have left your old home and not yet arrived in the new home of being awake. This is sleeping in the rain; this is suffering, this looking for home. And yet it is better, for those who have to do it, than trying to stay under the old roof that no longer shelters one from anything.

The second refuge is the *dharma. Dharma* has three meanings: truth, teaching, phenomena. So everything we encounter is *dharma*; all phenomena are teaching, all events are truth.

We take refuge in the truth. There is no shelter in lies or half-truths, but only in looking reality in the face. Here are grief, suffering, and impermanence, but also love. Here are fear, hope, and delight. All of human emotion, all of physical and mental pain is here; look at it. Do not pretend it is not real.

And finally we take refuge in the *sangha*, the community of believers or the community of practice. Traditionally *sangha* meant the community of monks, those who had taken vows and left home, who took up the robe and begging bowl and forsook ordinary ways of life. Now *sangha* is all those who have chosen the conscious life. So it is all humans and all beings.

Taking refuge in truth, in connection, in being awake, we are just here with each other in the inexpressible sweetness of the bonds that flow between us. Here I see a small being (who is any one of us) and a powerful web, a sweet and beautiful web, flowers and honey and the cream of the long river, the grasses that blow flowers in the field, the bees that travel among them.

Invitation

Release

Sit or lie comfortably. Close your eyes if you wish. Take a few deep breaths. If necessary, adjust your position so you are more comfortable.

With each in-breath, become aware that you are receiving the support of the universe.

With each out-breath, let go of tension and stress.

Inhaling, breathe in the sweetness of the air, of love and light, the beauty of all things. (If you wish, imagine yourself breathing in clear bright light or a dewlike morning mist.)

Exhaling, breathe out suffering, distress, fear, hopelessness; imagine them with heavy textures or dark colors if you like. Let them sink into the Earth, knowing that she receives us as we are, that she has the power to absorb and transmute our pain. Allow her embrace.

When you feel complete, focus your energy on the in-breath, experiencing it as energizing. Let the out-breath simply be stabilizing.

Take a few more breaths in this mode, then open your eyes and/or begin to move your body. Notice how you experience yourself and your surroundings at this moment.

Transformation

Sit comfortably erect, with your eyes closed or half open. Take a few breaths and, if necessary, shift your posture to be more balanced.

Now bring your attention to your in-breath. As you breathe in, be aware of all the pain and suffering in the world. Feel the cries of Earth's creatures . . . and take them into yourself. Breathing out, send sweetness and nourishment to all who need it.

Breathing in, take their sorrow into yourself. Breathing out, give love and healing.

Let your entire body become a crucible in which the suffering is transformed, purified, changed into love.

Remain in this mode as a source of healing until you are ready to return.

Now, with your next in-breath, simply breathe in, making no effort to take in anything except air. Breathe out, only air. Be aware again that your body is simply flesh and blood. Allow it to move a little, and open your eyes if they were closed. Notice the present state of your body, mind, energy.

Presence

Sit comfortably erect with your eyes open, your gaze relaxed. Take a few breaths, and if necessary shift your posture to be more balanced.

Breathe in, breathe out. Let your attention ride with the breath. Make no effort to change the breath; simply experience its movement in and out of your body. That which is vast, the air, enters your body and takes on a form. That which is form, your breath, returns to the universe and becomes vast. Sweetness circulates within and without, enters you and returns without. The sufferings of all beings become your own and yours flow into theirs. Intermingling, interpenetrating, you are both one with vast space and not-one, your own self.

Sit together in this way until you feel ready to stop. Then move your body slightly, then a little more. Notice how you experience yourself and your surroundings at this moment.

4

When You're the Other

> *I am defined as other in every group I'm a part of. The outsider, both strength and weakness. Yet without community there is certainly no liberation, no future, only the most vulnerable and temporary armistice between me and my oppression.*
> —AUDRE LORDE, *THE CANCER JOURNALS*
>
> *How different . . . our lives together would have been if we had known that we were not strangers in the world, having to invent and discover our purposes entirely on our own and from what we could learn from each other, pull out of each other in bewilderment and strife.*
> —JUDY GRAHN, *ANOTHER MOTHER TONGUE: GAY WORDS, GAY WORLDS*

The Ugly Duckling

In the story of "The Ugly Duckling," the duckling is ridiculed by peers, is rejected and runs away, is clumsy, tries to fit in but can't. He tries to survive alone and is forced repeatedly to find warmth wherever he can; he is grateful to be tolerated and finally has to leave anyway. He is filled with longing when he sees his own kind in the distance but finds it very, very difficult to recognize himself as a swan even when others do. Finally, as his true and beautiful nature emerges, the whole world comes into harmony.[8]

The duckling was unable to hide his difference, although he had no idea that it carried a gift for himself or others. Trying to conform, he failed; giving up, he was alone and miserable.

There is sometimes a temptation to misunderstand this story, to hear in it a suggestion that if you are mocked, it means you are better than the ones who scorn you. This misreading—this turn toward elitism—is actually a futile raging against the suffering of being alone, an emotionally expensive alternative to feeling ashamed, to blaming yourself for having no home and no people.

The real value of the ugly duckling story is in its offering of hope and its acknowledgment that our true nature is beautiful. It describes the journey we all experience when we open to unknown aspects of ourselves. At the same time it acknowledges the paths of people who don't fit any of the available cultural molds. And it identifies just how important this is: when the ugly duckling at last joins his people, it is then possible for the rest of the world to be whole.

For the duckling, once he's made it through the winter, spring comes. But not everyone makes it to spring. Some die; some lie locked in addictions; some find a way to survive by the hearth and never step outdoors again to have their hearts burst open in joy. Some reject those who have hurt them and spend their lives lonely in an inner winter.

Yet the promise is that if you survive and watch, the *possibility* is there. Your own beautiful self will grow, you may find your people, you will be part of the harmony of all.

Two tasks are named in this story: first, to survive, and second, to recognize our people when we finally find them. The promised result is that we will belong—not just among those who are like us, but among the whole of existence.

So we begin with survival. Sometimes this includes selling out for the sake of physical existence, but it always, somehow, requires keeping the faith deep inside. When roles were more rigid, how many women became secretaries instead of scientists, and how many men became engineers instead of dancers because these were approved occupations and because they needed to earn a living somehow? How many people of mixed blood abandoned their minority race when the possibility of "passing" presented itself to them? How many gay or transgender people passed for straight; how many changed clothes because it was easier to lie about their physical nature than about their internal workings? We seek shelter wherever it can be found.

Part of survival may be rebellion: to say "I am not this but that"—or sometimes, merely "I am not this." Many years ago, as a young full-time mother, I agonized over what to write as my occupation on the tax form. I felt that to write "housewife" or "homemaker" even once would have been an act of fundamental betrayal of myself. Once I wrote "mother" to emphasize that my ordinary woman's life had value just as it was. But the next year I wrote "unemployed," defiantly insisting that my real calling was something else, though I did not yet know what it was.

Having rejected or failed at the role that we were raised to fill, our next task is to find or define another.

Looking for my own place, I moved three times in one year, quit jobs, joined political organizations and communal households, hitchhiked around the country, entered therapy—and despaired that I would never belong anywhere.

Neither the time I spent with other lesbians nor my involvement in women's spirituality satisfied this need, because the need was inside of me. I needed a spiritual identity, not merely a group where I was accepted; and I needed spiritual space not only as a woman, not even just as a lesbian. I needed space as *myself.*

Each one of us needs no less.

I eventually had to learn that it was inside myself that the space needed to be found.

We all are looking for what we may have forgotten about how to be human; how to be woman, man, both, or neither; how to be child, adult, or elder. In ordinary life it is in myth that we find our spiritual identities named and affirmed. If we do not find ourselves in the stories and myths of childhood, we must look elsewhere as adults.

Quite without knowing what my fascination was about, during grade school I devoured tales of Norse gods and heroes and in high school turned to science fiction and fantasy, finding in both places a few stories of daring and adventurous women to dream on.

As an adult I looked in cultural anthropology for my place in real history. There were hints in Joseph Campbell, Mircea Eliade, and others, but it was with Judy Grahn's *Another Mother Tongue: Gay Words, Gay Worlds,* that I actually started to feel like there was a place for me in the human community. Grahn connected the old stories, the rumors of how we had once been a part of it all, with modern American gay life. She offered a spiritual identity that I recognized. She put names and faces on my yearning discontent, and invited company into the lonely room of my heart.

And so, among women I knew, this book became something to be talked about, passed along to anyone who was searching. "Here is water, here is life," we said to each other. "Here is my story, written and heard. Now I have a place, now I can exist, now I can be human." And when we heard it from each other, we knew again that we were not alone—for each person who responded in the same way was another one of us.

We all wonder where we belong, as the structures shift around us. Some of us reexamine traditional myths, old stories, and fairy tales; some practice ancient ceremonies and old religions. Some of us create new religions and write new myths. Looking in the face of chaos, we seek structures that free rather than bind us. We prefer what has stood the test of time but will create if need be.

For years after finding a myth that made sense of my life, I was obsessed with it. I talked about it, wrote about it, wanted everyone to understand just how important this was. Most people did not agree; many simply didn't care.

The rest of life continued. I gradually discovered that people liked me for who I was; like the ugly duckling turned swan, I was amazed. I didn't have to earn my place through brilliant scholarship or demand it by dire predictions that the culture would stagnate and die without me and my kind.

Finally I became able to listen to those who said "let go," to realize they were not all saying "shut up."

This is the last task: to let the myth slip into the background and let life proceed on its course.

Once we've recognized our place, we can stop fighting for the right to exist. Life welcomes us regardless of role or meaning.

Heyoka

A great wind blows across the sky. One person stands in that wind, breathes it, catches it, becomes it. That person channels it for the benefit of the people, bringing the vast sweep of clean air down to the ground, translating it into words or actions that can be comprehended by the human mind.

That person must stand in the wind, liking it or not; that person, like it or not, must bring it into the community. That person is called *heyoka* by the Lakota.[9]

"*Heyoka*" means "contrary." It is a difficult role—not desired or envied, but respected among the people who named it. A young person may discover this role at puberty, during a vision quest. There may be other ways to realize it as well.

The one who is heyoka (and the whole community knows who it is) has certain obligations. The heyoka will have certain dreams that must be acted out for the benefit of the group. No matter how ridiculous or embarrassing the actions in the dream, the heyoka *must* do them and the community *must* pay attention.

The role of heyoka comes with a responsibility, a heavy one. The responsibility is to hear the message of the spirits accurately and to convey it to the community in a way that can be heard. If people won't listen, the heyoka must find another way to communicate the message. Heyoka also can bear enormous grief when they are not heard.

Take Up Your Life

Like a tornado, the great wind that is heyoka can burst through barriers, tear down walls, and then demand rebuilding. It aims at what is old and encrusted. The individual who is heyoka brings its message, pointing at what needs to be taken down or swept away. If people will attend to the message, the wind can remain gentle.

It happens everywhere that institutions need to be torn down, old ways changed. It happens everywhere that individuals are born to carry the message, to channel the wind. But it does not happen everywhere that the one who carries the message is heard and heeded.

To be heyoka in a culture where everyone knows, acknowledges, and understands the role is hard enough. To be heyoka where no one knows, where to carry the wind's voice is to be considered crazy or an enemy, is much harder. It causes great pain, loneliness, and even self-destruction.

If you are heyoka, you are an integral part of the community—regardless of how alienated you feel.

In the unrecognized state, heyoka's close companion is self-doubt. The first challenge for every unrecognized heyoka is to distinguish whether the message is a true spirit message or mere personal contrariness.

Self-doubt can best be taken as an ally whose job it is to keep you honest. If it is not an ally, it can defeat you. Better then to treat it as an ally and insist that it act like one.

The second challenge is to communicate effectively, in a way that will be heard. In modern Western culture, we don't have an audience that knows who we are or that will assume we carry a message from beyond. No: here we have an audience that usually assumes that there *is* no beyond, and no spirits, and no messages.

And the third challenge is to continue. Not to run away, not to hate, not to take as a personal rejection every failure to communicate your message. The challenge is to not shut up, to not be silenced.

If you are heyoka, you are part of the community, like it or not. *You do not get to leave.* Seclusion, rest, reprieve, healing—yes. Leaving, abandoning, giving up—no.

Maledoma Some, in writing about community and spirit, refers to people who have "gone private." Someone who has gone private has emotionally or psychically left the community. While still physically present, such an individual has withheld magical or sacred powers to use strictly for individual ends. Such a person is thus a danger to others and must be guarded against.[10]

Sometimes the heyoka, like the hermit or the political rebel, can be mistaken for such a person. But the heyoka must also guard against *becoming* such a person. Bitterness can be a reaction to rejection, and it must never gain control.

The failure of a heyoka to meet these requirements can be dramatic. Addiction, criminality, suicide, and mental illness claim their share of unrealized heyokas.

Your life is not your own. This is true for everyone, yet it is put to the test more often and more vividly for a person who carries heyoka energy.

There is no choice but to act with love.

Silence

My silences had not protected me. Your silence will not protect you. But for every real word spoken, for every attempt I had ever made to speak those truths for which I am still seeking, I had made contact.
—AUDRE LORDE, THE CANCER JOURNALS

When I lived in a small town in a culture other than my own, my straight friends advised me not to tell anyone that I was a lesbian. They all said to me, "You can be yourself without being out."

I tried it, or thought I did. I didn't talk about any of the parts of me that I thought would get me in trouble. I looked elsewhere for safe places to take those parts, to talk without fear, to give them air. And so my heart was always somewhere else. Somehow, meaning to join the community in which I lived, I spent all my time alone.

And somehow, meaning to stay out of trouble, I found ways to always be in trouble. Time after time I found myself making amends for things I had said or done that seemed crazy even to me. Trying to protect myself in one arena, I found ways to destroy myself in others. I could not understand why.

I alienated half my support system, wore out half the others, and became afraid to ask anything from those who remained because my need seemed overwhelming. It was the loneliest time I've ever known.

I became ever more isolated. I took frequent trips away, to a place where I could be openly who I was. I came up with a series of personal projects that kept me busy in my spare time. I read intensively about the culture in which I lived, rather than participate in it.

I had gone there to be a psychotherapist—to help others. I did my job as well as I could, making occasional earnest mistakes along the way. And I did have friends, a few of whom knew. Those few became enormously important to me. And, yes, I did find one other lesbian, and one gay man—and quickly developed antagonisms with both of them. (This is a pattern observed among minorities of all kinds under similar conditions.)

My whole life became work, the work of how to live in that place. And I didn't ask for the help I needed, because I was afraid if I went to a warm, friendly place I would let my guard down and tell the secret. I did not want to find out whether my friends would abandon me once they knew.

Once or twice I made a fool of myself in public: the need to be seen for who I was would not be denied, and when I tried to suppress it, it came out and sabotaged me.

When I finally admitted my isolation and attempted to close my exits, simply by staying in town for three consecutive months, I fell sick and spent two weeks in bed with a mysterious illness that left me unable to work, to be active, or even to read.

Keeping my secrets, I never entered that community.

If you have a secret, you become the walls you erect to hide it.

Some people claim to be able to put away parts of themselves and function with the rest. But human beings exist in community, not alone. To the extent that we have a secret—a secret we believe we absolutely cannot tell—we are not in community and thus lose a bit of our humanness.

This is true of any secret, of any kind. Not just gays and lesbians, not just people of color passing as white, not just people who've done a deed in the past they think could never be forgiven, not just people nursing terrible anger over the wounds of racism, sexism, classism, ableism, any ism. And not just people who think they're superior and also think that this very sense of superiority is an unforgivable sin. All of us are made less by the secrets we keep within walled places.

There's something especially wounding if those secrets have to do with our life force, our personal expression, what we hold dearest to our hearts. If we experience ourselves as living in a culture hostile to what makes us who we are, the wound cuts deep.

Yet it's too simple just to say "Tell." First of all, it might be dangerous. Second, not everyone needs to know. Your intensely important secret may be a distraction from your real business with someone. And dealing with the consequences of telling may be a distraction from your real business with your own life.

We need to find a place between secrecy and complete public revelation. Finding it can be difficult. It is also our obligation—to ourselves and to the others with whom we would be in community.

Back in our dreamtime culture, the place where people truly

know how to use and appreciate those who are different, you don't have a secret to tell because everybody knows who you are. The space is there for you, and you can step into it.

In a broken culture, one that ignores or ridicules the heyoka, the different one, the space is also there. Only it is surrounded by fear—fear that the different ones will destroy the community. Because the community is weak and its bonds are fragile, it cannot afford to give space to those who would change it. It cannot even distinguish between destructive forces and forces for positive change.

For each of us who is different, the question is how to be part of the community, how to have and cherish our differences without needing to push them in people's faces. This is so difficult because it is the very pressure to be quiet—to keep our identities partly or entirely secret—that drives so many of us to become overly outspoken or even militant.

To be in community, we have to reach across the interminable gulf without denying that the gulf is there. We cannot reach each other if we pretend the other is somewhere (or someone) else. This is true regardless of which side we are reaching from.

When we can reach each other, healing becomes possible. There is healing when someone sees and affirms you exactly as you are, without trying to deny your history or your pain.

We also have to remember that there is no such thing as a complete outsider. Each of us shares something with the majority, even if it seems trivial. And there is probably no such thing as a complete insider. (Or if there is, these people make up the most exclusive club on Earth.) The rest of us live on both sides at once.

Those of us whose differences are not dangerous to ourselves—who have never been punished by exile, imprisonment, enslavement, or death—must acknowledge our position of safety, must consider what kind of community we want, must look out across the gulf, must build the bridge.

Keep Your Own Mind

The Dalai Lama was asked why he wasn't angry with the Chinese. They had taken his country and were destroying its culture, killing his people, and desecrating the temples of Tibet.

He replied, "They've taken all that, and you think I should let them take my mind as well?"

Do not cooperate with greed or hatred. Be loving, be kind, be compassionate, without giving in. Do not cooperate with abuse or oppression.

When you enter into rage or antagonism toward people or organizations that commit injustice, you are cooperating with injustice. When you keep your self clear, your own mind and heart calm, then you have the possibility of not cooperating. Knowing who you are, you can choose to do something else.

The first step, this turning, is the same for all of us. All the rest you have to invent on your own.

— Take Up Your Life —

Invitation

Read!

Read. Read poetry, biography, fiction written by your own people, by the ones who know you best. Find the writers who write your life into existence. Go to the library or the bookstore; browse intensely.

When you find someone who tells your truth, get that book, take it home, keep it close to you. Paste quotations on your walls. Let the authors support you; out of their struggle draw your own spiritual and emotional food.

Read authors who are as like you as you can possibly find. Read, listening for your life. And then read some authors who are different. There's no telling where the magic will appear.

And if you don't find your own story anywhere, write it yourself. Get a notebook or journal and write your own life into existence. If you use a computer, print out your words so that they won't get lost and so you can see them, touch them, and read them anytime.

If you are ashamed of what you've written, keep it anyway. Shame often surrounds our important secrets. No matter what, read it next month. Or have someone who loves you read it aloud to you. Listen to your own story, and let in its truth and drama.

Grief Ritual

Think about the way the world looked to you when you were a child. What kind of life did you expect for yourself? What did you think was true for most people in the world? When did you first become aware of poverty, war, cruelty? In your own life or in the world, when did the dreams start to die? Gently remember the times in your life when you first realized how hard life can be or how often it is hard. Remember when you saw the limits in your own life. Whether you were three or thirty, recall the loss of illusion and the awareness of limits. Be as clear as possible. If it helps, make a written list.

Now, for each lost illusion, find a tangible symbol. It could be as simple as a rock or a leaf, a newspaper article, a poem, a photo—anything that represents to you the lost vision of the world.

Go to a special place—a private place in your home or a beautiful place outdoors—someplace where you can have some quiet time and where you will not be interrupted. If it's at home, turn off the phone or get someone else to answer it.

Place the symbols you have selected before you and look at them.

Now, speak to your lost illusions, one by one. If possible, hold or look at the symbol and speak aloud. Say what it meant to you, how you felt on losing it, and how you are living without it. Say good-bye to it . . . and then release it from your heart.

At the same time, release the material symbol of the dream in some way. Burn it, bury it, toss it to the wind or into a stream, leave it among the grasses or beside a tree.

If tears or anger arise, let them come. Take the time you need to admit your losses.

If you find yourself feeling like the child you once were—hopeless, helpless, or hysterical—maintain your steadiness by mentally following your breath. Pay attention to its movement in and out. Also notice your physical body as it contacts the ground or floor. Stay with your present physical sensations, and from that steadiness feel and accept the emotions of the child inside you. This is the hard work of the ritual.

When you are finished with the good-byes, return to your inner place of calm and centeredness. Focus on your breath, your awareness of your physical body, the beautiful or natural objects around you—whatever helps you remember that beauty and strength are still in the world. Stay in this place for a while. Here your adult self is making ready its response to the world as it is, without illusion. Consciously or not, something is gestating inside you. Give it room.

When you are ready, finish the ritual in whatever way seems right to you, and leave your special space for now.

Suggestions

- Deal with only a few subjects at one time. If you find yourself making long lists of lost dreams, either consolidate them into groups or set aside a time each day or each week to do a grief ritual, until you have let go of everything on your list.

- If one particular loss is very important to you, or if you are unable to finish with it, give it a separate ritual. Writing about it or talking with someone may also be helpful.

- If your symbol for a loss is a precious or sacred object, you may not want to lose it in the symbolic releasing. Make a copy or facsimile instead and use that in your ritual.

- If you can share this ritual with someone—a group, a friend, a lover or partner—do so. To share grief is to heal it further. If you have no such companions, don't wait; if it saddens you to do the ritual alone, honor that grief along with the others.

5

The Human Condition

> *All that is subject to arising is subject to cessation.*
>
> —*The Life of the Buddha*,
> Trans. Bhikkhu Nanamoli

Darkness

There is an old joke about a man searching frantically under a streetlamp. To a passing stranger he says urgently, "I've lost a priceless jewel that's been in my family for generations. Will you help me find it?"

The stranger begins to search as well, with no luck, and finally asks, "Are you sure this is where you lost it?"

The man replies, "No, I lost it over there in the alley."

Baffled, the stranger asks, "Then why are you searching for it here?"

"Well, the light is much better here."

We laugh; but perhaps we ought to cry.

We do not see that *we* are the ones who search where it is easy to search, rather than where the lost treasure may actually be found.

Seeking relief from violence, our nation—with the world's highest prison population—rejects preventive measures aimed at children, and instead approves more money for police and prisons.

Seeking relief from the wounds of an emotionally abusive childhood, an adult may look incessantly through self-help books and programs or stay endlessly in therapy, but refuse to reenter the place where the wound occurred: ordinary personal relationship.

We want to stay in the light, to stay where we think we know what is going on. We want to be in control; we want protection against harm. The darkness of night has always served as cover for animals and people who would attack us. Our bodies remember, if our minds sometimes do not, that literal darkness brings danger.

Psychic darkness is another matter. We still cannot see; we cannot control. And so we are afraid.

Yet grace and forgiveness dwell here, in this darkness, this wilderness beyond the realm of control.

If we ever hope to regain our lost jewels—which may be faith, hope, love, or any spiritual or emotional treasure—we need to venture into the dark. When we do, we are not entering the heavy shadows of evil but rather the darkness of the unknown. We must first gather a bit of strength and self-confidence and then take a first step in the very direction that is most uncertain and often most frightening.

To leave the known area, to remove our armor and venture out into the darkness, requires either total despair over our present life or a great trust that the darkness is indeed only one face of a compassionate universe.

Shame

I remember a line I memorized in grade school: *"visiting the iniquities of the fathers upon the children unto the third and fourth generations,"*[11] Shame is passed down from one generation to another, helplessly transmitted by parents who want to love their children but do not know how.

Shame hides from the present. It cannot hear words spoken in love, but it magnifies criticism a thousandfold. The person in its power cries, "You don't understand me!" while secretly fearing that you do, and that she or he is truly worthless and despicable.

Shame both seeks and fears the sunlight. It asks to be seen and loved in spite of itself, and when love appears it puts on its ugliest face to test whether the love is real. It seeks what it did not have before: unconditional love.

The condition of shame closes the emotional eyes and ears of people it has entrapped. It creates a condition of deep distrust of other people, who may see, mock, and abuse them; and also of themselves, fearing they may actually deserve the abuse.

Shame asks the question "Am I truly less than human, as they have told me?" Someone who has fully accepted the shame answers yes and learns to put up with more or less constant pain, apologizing for existing and attempting to correct the perceived faults. An individual who has only partially accepted the shame may be tormented by a great inner debate.

The image of self created by shame is persistent. And it is isolated, even though it wishes for community. Because of this wish, and because shame blocks the awareness that we *all* naturally belong in this world, a person in the grip of shame is at the mercy of the actions and attitudes of others—who can include or exclude the person in a hundred small and large ways. This dependence leads naturally to fear, and then to anger.

Here we have Buddhism's "three poisons" of greed, anger, and self-delusion: desperately wanting inclusion and acceptance (greed), while resenting one's own perceived helplessness (anger), and creating and maintaining a self-image as either unworthy or victimized (self-delusion).

Shame brings a need for control. A constant but familiar misery can seem easier to live with than the unknown and changing nature of the real world.

The biblical passage quoted earlier describes shame; but the passage in full names its cure: "I the Lord thy God am a jealous God, visiting the iniquities of the fathers upon the children unto the third and fourth generations of them that hate me, and *showing mercy unto thousands of them that love me and keep my commandments.*"[12]

The choice between mercy and the generational curse simply has to do with whether one loves or hates God. Welcome God—the healing power, the divine—into your life and you live with mercy. Shut it out, and your shame fills your own life and passes down to your children as well. Repent, move away from shame into love and forgiveness, and you are *immediately* in mercy.

Take Up Your Life

The teaching, received fully, is not about a jealous god but about the difficult reality of life. Hope lies in the very thing that is most difficult—letting go.

Six States

The samurai was a powerful and famous warrior, accustomed to being acknowledged with respect, if not reverence. He came to the Zen master with this request: "Please teach me about heaven and hell."

Instead of talking about either, the master began to ridicule him. "Look at you! You're not worthy to be a samurai at all. Your clothes are dirty, your carriage lopsided, your demeanor shameful." He went on and on until the samurai, filled with rage, raised his sword to cut the old man in two.

Suddenly the master stopped, pointed at him, and said, "That is hell."

The samurai, being of quick mind, immediately understood. He was filled with immense gratitude for this man who had risked his own life to teach him the meaning of hell. He put down the sword, knelt, and bowed deeply.

The master said simply, "That is heaven."

One day when I was struggling with anger, my friend Evangeline told me this story. Her concluding words were "Anger is hell. Gratitude is heaven. You choose."

States of mind are transient. We pass in and out of them like walking through the rooms of a house. And, as in a complex house, a map or floor plan can be helpful.

In Buddhist psychology, consciousness is divided into six general states: hell, the animal realm, the "hungry ghost" realm, the realm of fighting spirits, the god realm, and the human realm. What follows is a brief, unofficial tour of these six states as I understand them.

The Animal Realm

The animal state is always about survival. Consider, when you come upon a deer in the woods, how startled it looks, how quickly it bounds away to safety. Or consider the times when you've turned on a light in a badly maintained building. Remember how hurriedly the mice, rats, or cockroaches scurried for cover?

The life of an animal revolves around food and safety; if freed temporarily from fear, the animal sleeps.

Recently I was alone at night in a cabin where there had been a series of recent burglaries. I lay awake with a borrowed gun and my own fear. There was no question that I could defend myself against a possible intruder. Still, I could not sleep. I lay awake for hours, becoming uncomfortably intimate with my own fear. I watched where it lay in my body, how it speeded up my breath and raced through my veins, how a thought would rouse it again and wake me just as I was falling asleep. Finally, convinced that it would do its job and wake me if needed, I let go of the extras and slept.

Letting go of fear means trusting it to do its proper job: alerting us in case of danger. That is what fear is for, just as physical pain informs us that our bodies are being damaged. Both fear and pain share a purpose: mobilizing us into action.

The deer needs its fear in order to escape the hunter. In the same way, we need fear, on occasion, to alert us to situations of danger. But we do not need to live continually in fear, ready to flee or fight at any moment.

The other predominant characteristic of the animal state is the constant, boring search for food. This impulse also arises appropriately in us. It is necessary to care for our bodies' need for food and shelter. It is *not* necessary—or healthy—to continue this effort once we've obtained a reasonable amount of each (plus reasonable security for future needs). Yet how often do we live in this state, either going to a boring job day after day or constantly on the alert for a new opportunity, when something less is at stake?

To live with a grinding, wearing sense of need is one thing when it is real. But an enormous number of people live exhausting animal-realm lives when in fact their basic needs are being met. A nice home (plus a vacation cottage), a new car (or two cars plus a boat and snowmobile), an expensive resort vacation (or ongoing major expenditures on "personal growth" workshops), quality clothes (or a second closet full)—are any of these actually needs? Even intangibles such as influence, prestige, status, and fame can seem like essentials for survival.

To turn luxuries into wants is to live in spiritual poverty. It is to seek what no longer needs to be sought; it is to choose the animal realm of fear and survival; it is to make ourselves smaller and less alive than we actually are.

Choose a balance; choose what you will define as necessity, and what you will keep but enjoy as luxury: Choose in what way you wish to live. Doing so, you move out of the animal realm and into the realm of human life: the realm where work, love, spirituality, and meaning can be found.

The Hungry Ghost Realm

In Buddhist mythology, the hungry ghost is a being with an enormous, distended belly and a neck so thin that very little can pass down it. This is the realm of wanting, wanting, and never being able to be filled.

If you offer food to a hungry ghost, it won't be enough, or it will be the wrong thing. You offer it steak, and it says, "I'm a vegetarian." You offer it rice and it says, "What I really need right now is a salad" (or a chocolate bar). If you offer comfort and love, it thinks you are lying; a hungry ghost cannot trust. And so forth: whatever the hungry ghost needs, it cannot have. Hungry ghost people are very hard to be around.

If you've known a "needy" person—the modern term for the hungry ghost—you could see the problem was in their skinny-necked inability to receive. But if you've ever been in this state yourself—utterly alone, unwanted, rejected, poor, sick, abandoned, unemployed, or seemingly without a resource in the world—it's a little harder to see the narrowness of your own throat.

The hungry ghost realm is where you go when you've latched onto emotional or material poverty as a way of life. It's a miserable state. It drives people away from you; it perpetuates itself. People run away from hungry ghosts, fearing that their constant need will suck them dry.

The ways out of the hungry ghost realm are few and difficult: to accept and appreciate what is offered to you; to make the effort to believe that the universe will support and respond to your efforts; to look for blessings in your situation; or to just wake up and let go of your desperation. Each of these requires you to act in contradiction to your immediate experience, which is why they are so hard to do.

Another, more indirect route out is via the animal realm. Learn to accept a half or quarter of what you want; learn the difference between need and want and settle for what you need. Once you have experienced having what you need, you have found the doorway out of the hungry ghost realm. From there you can go on.

However, another often-chosen route leads from the hungry ghost straight into the hell-realms. Here you replace "I'm not good enough" and "I never have enough" with "They hurt me" or "They are unjust." What you're holding onto is anger—at the parents who didn't raise you well enough or at a group that treats you and yours unfairly. Anger may be a path out of the miserable situation of lack, want, and despair. Add moral superiority and you can walk right into the addictive state of righteous anger.

The only thing better about anger is this: in anger you have some sense of power. Thus, when you finally get tired of hell, you may be able to use that power to leave. What's worse is this: that anger carries its own forms of satisfaction. You may find it attractive and fulfilling enough to stay stuck in it.

And yet there is another way out. It is possible to wake up directly, to say "This is where I am, and I don't want to be here." Cultivating gratitude is such a path.

To pay attention to what's good, to appreciate a sunrise or a nourishing meal or a smile from a stranger, without immediately launching into the familiar internal refrain on why it's not enough—this may help. To seek professional help, ignoring the internal complaint about having to pay for what ought to come naturally through friendships—this may help.

As a starting place, it can help to get fully acquainted with the internal complaint—to listen to it attentively, compassionately, and nonjudgmentally—until you are truly and wholeheartedly tired of it. Then you can make your move.

For a while—perhaps a long while—it may seem impossible to turn off the tapes; it may seem like the problem really is outside you rather than within you; it may seem like you just can't see the way out.

Until, suddenly, there it is right in front of you, and you wonder why you couldn't see it before.

The Hell Realm

Anger, like fear, is an ancient physiological protective mechanism. It brings us immediately to alertness, ready to fight for our lives if necessary. Muscle tension, adrenaline, and hypersensitivity are all parts of this survival tool.

Anger does have a place in ordinary life: it can help us to act decisively when physical safety is at stake. Its appropriate duration is exactly as long as needed for survival and safety. Often it appears as a spontaneous outburst; it defends, protects, challenges, sets things right, or sweeps them clean; it vanishes as quickly as it came.

When anger stays beyond its needed role, we move into the hell realm. Then the voice of anger may sound something like this: *You don't respect me. You don't care about me. People are bad; why can't they be good like me? I'm going away by myself. . . .*

Notice how many of these sentences end with "me"? Anger is always about I, me, and mine.

Anger can expand; it can reach out to include your family

(against the obnoxious neighbors), your race or ethnic group (against the majority or against a specific enemy), your country as you imagine it (against immigrants, African Americans, Jews, homosexuals, and a host of other groups), your union (against the bosses), your children (against an unfair schoolteacher), or you and your lover against the whole world.

The word *against* is the clue that tells us that anger is here. What matters is not who is being included but whether anyone is being excluded. It does *not* matter whether the excluded person or group actually has done something to trigger the anger; anger held onto is a poison no matter how legitimate its source.

In anger, the other person or group becomes less than human. This is exactly the perspective you'd need if you were going to protect your life by disabling your attacker. It's not a good way to live.

The more important we think we are, the more easily we can get angry. The more disconnected we are, the faster rage can rise. "Righteous" anger in particular comes with arrogance—believing that I know more than someone else, that I should be in charge, that I would do it right. In righteous anger I'm all-important and raging at those who don't recognize that fact. Righteous anger carries a satisfaction that can make hell tolerable for a long time.

Anger has a sense of power in it. Often this is what draws people to it. But there is a power greater than anger. It arises from compassion and gives rise to seeming miracles, as when a small woman finds the strength to lift a car off her baby. This is a power that remains connected both with other humans and with the divine.

To get out of hell, you have to notice you are there—and that there is somewhere else to go.

Unfortunately, many people choose to move from anger into the realm of the fighting spirits.

The Realm of Fighting Spirits

This realm is all about the game of competition. Fighting spirits are competitive, jealous, greedy. They enjoy—and can become powerful at—a certain kind of politics or business. Fighting spirits are also attracted to street gangs or drug wars. Often they find their place in mixing up families to create conflict and disharmony, promoting pettiness in churches or social service organizations, or competing for praise, attention, awards, power, and property. Fighting spirits look for angles, opportunities for personal benefit or advancement, and someone to blame or someone to exploit.

Here is the excitement of the fight, whether that fight is for personal economic success or for class, race, or ideology. Here life is not dull but full of crises and fraught with enemies.

To leave this realm you have to get tired of crisis, exhausted from the struggle, or perhaps lonely. Or you can have an attack of conscience, because in this state the harm you do to others usually will be quite visible—to them at least, if not always to you.

To work for justice without getting caught in this realm, without forgetting the humanness of your opponent, without indulging in righteous anger or moral superiority—to do so is to dissolve your own internal fighting spirit in favor of the spirit of love and compassion. To have any chance of doing this requires constant awareness.

The God Realm

Devas or gods are beautiful, happy, powerful, and smugly satisfied with themselves. The reason to avoid this state is that it doesn't—and can't—last forever.

And when it starts to fall apart (your economic empire disintegrates, you fall from grace with your employer, your lover goes off with another, your students accuse you of sexual harassment), there's hope for waking up. There also may be serious temptation to commit suicide at this point, because in this state you don't learn many of the survival skills needed in ordinary life.

The God realm, like all of the others except the human realm, is yet another form of unconsciousness.

The Human Realm

In all of the five previous realms *you* are the center of your own attention. In the human realm you can notice this and then grow out of it. Instead of being a prisoner of I, me, and mine, you start to develop the ability to step out of that small place, to notice the world around you, to view your life in perspective. What we call maturity and responsibility belong in the human realm.

The definition of the human realm is simply this: self-awareness. Only in the human realm are we able to laugh at ourselves. Only here do we have the ability to wake up, to get beyond

Take Up Your Life

ordinary existence and leave suffering behind. And only as human beings can we fully engage in the great struggle: to love and be loved.

≈

These six states are like rooms in a house: we walk from one into another, sometimes thinking we've escaped, only to find the next state equally oppressive, painful, or difficult. Still, it can take a long time to recognize the new misery, because we're so glad to be done with the old.

There are various routes through the varieties of suffering. But anger is always hell, fear is always animal, and helpless loneliness is always the hungry ghost. The states become filters, so we don't see other people as just other people or ourselves as just another person.

Sometimes you can just step out of one of these states directly into the human. Responsibility, guilt, and self-examination *in moderation* all can bring us to humanness. But it's easy to go overboard or to slide back. Trying desperately to change, trying to get mentally healthier as quickly as possible, can be a hungry ghost activity; you try your hardest to get *out* of that miserable state, but your very effort is what keeps you there.

So what to do? Pay attention, stay awake to what you're doing, and keep paying attention. When you put what you're thinking and doing together with how you feel, you may find the ability to let go of the thoughts that cause pain. Each state, each room in the house, is a mind-set. Getting out of it is as simple as flicking a switch—if only you knew the switch was there. This is why people say "Just snap out of it"—and why others look at them like they're crazy.

It's said that only from the human realm can you move into enlightenment.

The Three Poisons

Greed, hate, and self-delusion; lust, anger, and ignorance: the three poisons go by many names, but they define the three essential causes of human suffering.

Greed or lust looks upon another person (or a thing) with the aim to take it, incorporate it, use it. Greed ignores any qualities of consciousness, humanness, or sacredness in anything but itself.

Hate or anger looks upon the other person or thing with the intention of destroying it, sending it away, or hurting it. Dislike and revenge are both aspects of this poison. It, like greed, ignores any values or experiences the other may have, considering only its own yearnings and wants.

Ignorance, self-delusion, illusion—a failure to understand deeply our true nature. In its deepest and most common form, it is the illusion that we are separate from each other. Unaware that we are profoundly connected, we are able to hurt, use, or abuse each other. Acting as if we are separate from each other, we intensify the illusion of separation and increase our ability to harm each other.

What is the antidote for these poisons? We must act as though we are *not* separate from each other—which is acting in accordance with reality. When we do this we open the possibility of experiencing connection with other people, with all the world, and with what we call God.

Invitation

Exploring Anger

It's best to do this meditation briefly the first time, working your way into it gradually by repeating it over a period of several days or weeks. It may bring sadness, discomfort, revelation, or even all three. It may take some practice. If you find it difficult, simply do the best you can.

Sit in an alert yet comfortable position. Take several relaxed breaths.

Slowly, find your anger. If you are not angry now, let your mind recall a pattern of thought that usually brings up anger for you; stay with it until you experience some anger.

Now shift the focus of your awareness. Pay attention to your body and mind. Note how you are sitting—erect or slouched—and where tension resides in your body. Take some time with this, and do a complete inventory of your body without attempting to change anything. If other thoughts appear, simply allow them to arise and drift away at their own pace.

After you have checked in with your entire body, allow yourself to shift positions so that you are more comfortable physically. Let your attention float throughout your body; notice where tension lies. Gently let yourself know in which of these tense places there is anger, or resentment, or hate, or judgment, or rage.

Then, also gently, choose one of these areas and explore it in depth, again without attempting to change it. Get acquainted with the physical

> *expression of your anger. Is it hard, soft, brittle, flexible, warm, cool, pleasant, unpleasant, mobile, static, compressed, expansive? Consider that all these qualities belong to the anger that you call yours.*
>
> *Now, as if you were meeting someone new, investigate these qualities. Allow yourself to be curious, interested, dismayed, pleased, disappointed, excited, or surprised.*
>
> *At last, when you feel well enough acquainted, say hello to your anger. Welcome it into your being as you might welcome a stray cat or dog that's been hanging around your home. Think about how you will care for it, and what limits you will place upon it. As with a new pet, be aware that you may need to train it, sometimes with sternness.*
>
> *Take as much time as you like to imagine the role that this being—anger—will play in your life.*
>
> *When you are ready, return to an awareness of your body. Explore the same areas you did before, gently paying attention to qualities, textures, and shapes. How is this body now?*

If you still have difficulty after several repetitions, change to another meditation for a while and come back later.

Use this same meditation to explore each of the other poisons just described, or fear, need, pride, or any other emotion that causes you difficulty.

Embracing Forgiveness

Begin to reflect on the word "forgiveness." What does it mean? What might it be like to bring forgiveness into your life, into your heart?

Bring into your mind the image of someone for whom you have much resentment. Gradually allow a picture, a feeling, a sense of this person to gather there. Gently invite the person into your heart for just this moment.

Just be present with that image, experimenting with the truth of being with the person. Notice whatever fear or anger may arise to limit or deny her or his entrance. Gently let that fear or anger soften.

Then, silently in your heart, say to this person, "I forgive you."

Open further to a sense of the person's presence. Say again, "I forgive you for whatever pain you may have caused me in the past, intentionally or unintentionally, through your words, your thoughts, your actions. However you may have caused me pain in the past, I forgive you."

Don't judge yourself for how difficult it may be.

"I forgive you for whatever you may have done that caused me pain, intentionally or unintentionally, through your actions, through your words, even through your thoughts, through whatever you did or through whatever you didn't do. However the pain came to me through you, I forgive you. I forgive you."

Open to the person at your own pace. If it hurts, let it hurt. And open to your resentment and your anger, even if it burns.

"I forgive you."

Now bring into your heart the image of someone from whom you wish to ask forgiveness. Speak to the person in your heart: "I ask your forgiveness for anything I may have done in the past that caused you pain, either by my thoughts or my actions or my words. Even for those things I didn't intend to cause you pain, I ask your forgiveness. For all that came out of confusion, forgetfulness, or fear, I ask your forgiveness."

Don't let any resentment you hold for yourself block your reception of forgiveness. Let your heart soften to it. Allow yourself to be forgiven.

Let the unworthiness come up; let the anger at yourself come up; let it fall away; let yourself be freed.

Now bring yourself into your heart. Say "I forgive you" to yourself.

Using your own first name, in your heart say, "I forgive you." Open to that. Make room in your heart for yourself.

Let your resentments fall away. Let go of the bitterness, the hardness, the judgment of yourself. Allow your heart to open to you.

Feel the place of love and enter into it. Allow yourself the compassion, the care of self-forgiveness. Let yourself float gently in the open heart of understanding, of forgiveness, of peace.[13]

6

Hope

> *Fear not, for I have redeemed you; I have called you by name: you are mine. When you pass through the water, I will be with you; in the rivers you shall not drown. When you walk through fire, you shall not be burned; the flames shall not consume you.*
>
> —ISAIAH 43:1–2
>
> *Obey the nature of things (your own nature) and you will walk freely and undisturbed. . . . With a single stroke we are freed from bondage; nothing clings to us and we hold to nothing.*
>
> —SENG-TS'AN, SIXTH-CENTURY CHINESE ZEN MASTER, *THE HSIN HSIN MING*

Beyond Suicide

The urge to commit suicide usually arises because life is painful—unbearably, unremittingly painful without hope of change. People can endure great pain, but only if they believe it will end or if it is for a purpose.

There have been times when a whole people chose suicide. In Spain, facing conquest by conquering Roman armies, pre-Christian peoples waded into the sea en masse. In A.D. 73 a group of Jews in a fortress called Masada chose death over surrender to their enemies in combat.

In modern North America, under the subtler assaults on Native American civilization, here and there is a tribe or village where nearly every adult is alcoholic. In these places, the death rates from murder, suicide, and accident are astronomical. Fetal alcohol syndrome or its lesser sibling, fetal alcohol effect, claims a large proportion of the children; the victims must be watched and cared for even into adulthood and will likely never be contributing members of their communities. Their need for supervision and special care burdens both the generation responsible for leadership and the generation longing to retire. This is a slower way for a people to die.

And mainstream America—the conqueror—is going in the same direction. What can I say to show you, if you don't already know and feel it? Crime, drugs, violence on TV, soaring prison populations—while our youth, like all youth faced with death, engage in sex as if there were no risks and no tomorrow. They make babies as an instinctive, inadequate response to the death of spirit around them.

Yet there is hope.

One native tribe—riddled with alcoholism and its attendant disorders—came to the brink of death and turned back. In Alkali Lake, British Columbia, in 1972, alcoholism held sway over everyone past the age of seven. People talked about the problem, but they kept drinking.

Then, one day, a child refused to go home. This seven-year-old girl could not bear it any longer. That day her mother stopped drinking.

Soon she was joined by her husband.

After a lonely year and a half, with the support of only a single person from outside, they were joined by another, then another and another and another.[14]

Over the course of fifteen years this tribe moved, as a community, from the brink of cultural and emotional death to radiant, vibrant life.

It is never necessary to give up.

Going On

In Japan, up until World War II, there was a temple that included an ancient tree, venerated for generations. People held marriages under this tree, brought their children there for their first blessing, held funerals there. Daily offerings were made to the tree, and services and chanting were frequent. It was a beloved part of the community and was regarded as a source of blessing for all.

This temple was near the center of Hiroshima. The tree was killed when an atomic bomb was dropped on the city on August 6, 1945.

The people were dismayed, lost. They did not know what to do. How would their lives go on without the support of the beloved spirit that was their great tree?

Not knowing what to do, they continued their daily routine. They brought offerings of food and water to the tree, just as they had done when it was alive. They continued to hold their ceremonies under it, to pray to it, and to bring their lives into its presence. For forty-five years they continued in this manner with the dead tree.

And then, one spring, the tree brought forth flowers once again.

To take up a lost cause is to continue when despair is the only reasonable course.

This is where the opening occurs. This is hope.

One cannot hope that the tree will bloom. One cannot plan. Hope is not a belief that the continued acts of devotion will bring back the lost. No; if the offerings of the people of Hiroshima had been designed to that end, they would have been acts of magic or fantasy and not the true thing.

What, then, is hope?

Hope is in the present. It reaches out and embraces. It persists. It continues. It will not give up, even though reason says it ought to quit.

Hope greets life warmly. Hope focuses on life even when surrounded by death; it finds encouragement in the midst of suffering.

What we usually mean by hope is that we expect something specific to get better. This can help us through a rough moment, by postponing disappointment. But this kind of hope is false; it is actually a commitment to illusion. When things go badly, when we are disappointed again and again, any investment we have made here will become proof *against* hope, reason for cynicism, cause for despair.

There is another hope, one that actually can give us something that lasts. This hope means trusting that there's some kind of pattern, that difficulties have meaning, that our lives make sense.

This hope trusts that "all things work together for good for those that love God,"[15] even when it cannot understand the details of this present moment. Embraced by all beings, resting in the care of a benevolent God or a friendly universe, it knows that whatever happens is part of a process that works. This hope lets the larger forces do their job while we do ours.

The deepest level of hope comes when we let go of needing life to make sense. Here we find the possibility of replacing "Why me?" with "Why not me?" Embraced in the largeness of all life, we become willing to put up with difficulty, with pain and suffering, with uncertainty and confusion.

In this most spacious hope, expectations are simply irrelevant. We meet each day with warmth and enthusiasm. We embrace life as it is. We laugh compassionately at our own mistakes. Here, finally, we are able to say with Job, "The Lord giveth and the Lord taketh away; blessed be the name of the Lord."[16]

There's a story of a rabbi in the Nazi concentration camps. He was very hungry, as was everyone. He found a potato. Another man found him and tried to take it from him. They struggled. Suddenly he thought, "What am I doing, fighting with this man for a potato?" He remembered who he was; in that instant his life changed.

The fact that he survived to tell the story is not so important as what happened to him in that moment: that he remembered his larger self.

That people can remember themselves in surroundings designed to destroy their humanity: here is hope.

This brings us back to the story of the Hiroshima tree. It

seemed to those people that the tree, the source of blessing, the spiritual center, was dead. And they kept going.

When you keep going through despair, when you continue to bring the offerings even as you weep, it makes something in you alive. Continuing through despair, you feed the living place within that is hope, that knows life, that knows all is well in spite of appearances.

That is hope: the deep conviction—no, the choice—no, the *necessity*—to dwell in the knowledge that all is well. Dwelling here and in the world of sorrow and injustice together, you gradually become able to find that wellness beneath the surface of despair.

Then hope blooms in you like the tree coming to flower again, and the miracle blesses us all.

So What?

This story comes from an anonymous Zen student who was also a gay man. Unfortunately, his spiritual community did not fully accept homosexuals. As a result, he repeatedly suffered injustice and discrimination from his fellow Buddhists; yet he felt called to practice Zen.

One day he went to meet with a visiting teacher. He poured out his tale of woe. The teacher listened carefully but impassively. At last, when the story was over, the teacher said, "So what?" And the student was healed.

It's easy to get wrapped up in the injustices directed toward ourselves or those we love, or even those we don't know. It's a powerful distraction.

We'd all like to escape from the difficulties, hassles, indignities, and injustices of everyday life. But to be free from those difficulties, we need to be free *within* them. And that happens only when we accept that they are in our lives, are parts of our lives. It happens when we become willing to deal with them, day after day after day.

"So what?" Some people are born in Somalia, Bangladesh, Chile, and other places of anguish; some are born the "wrong" race, gender, or class; some are born to abusive or impoverished parents.

Some people simply have hard lives, without any noticeable choice in the matter. Others have it easy.

What big difference does it make which role I have in life? Whatever life I have, that is the one I must take care of. Whatever life I have, that is the one that takes care of me.

Breaking Open

My Zen teacher, Reb Anderson, said to me, "It's normal to get to a place where you feel like you can't go on."

When you seek healing, you need compassion, patience, and respect for yourself. You need a willingness to receive, to learn, to make mistakes and start again. You need to be open to companionship, even though it will be imperfect.

Healing involves welcoming your life: just going forward in your life no matter how hard it is or what it brings you. You let yourself feel what hurts; you let it in, you give up denial, and still you keep going.

"Find the present of your pain," says Reb. "Practice patience with it."

Eventually, going forward in this way, you come to a place where it has to break open. Or it breaks you open. Or you can tell that something has to break but you have no idea whether it is the inside or the outside that has to give. You want the thing outside to break, to let go, so you won't have to. You want the other people to change, or your body to miraculously recover, or the war to end, or your lost child to return to life; you want a job or a lover or whatever is missing to suddenly appear and rescue you from your suffering.

what we think is ours. We protect our life, our dignity, our relationships against all kinds of perceived threats. This is the foolishness of human nature; this is its eternal sorrow.

Before we can do anything, we must allow the grief to arise and flow.

Before we can offer anything, do anything, heal anything, we must receive, must be healed. Together.

Take Up Your Life

Invitation

Becoming the Holy

Sit comfortably erect, or lie with your spine fully supported, eyes closed. Take a few breaths, settling into your body and its present position.

When you are ready, bring your attention to the area in the center of your chest, to your heart. Feel the rise and fall of your chest as you breathe; feel or imagine the pulsing of your heart as it moves blood throughout your body. Become fully present with the miracle of your own body.

Now imagine within your heart a being the size of your thumb. Give this being the name of the being holiest to you—Jesus, Buddha, Muhammad, Kwan Yin, Tara, Ishtar, Shiva, White Buffalo Woman, Avalokitesvara. Imagine this being—the embodiment of love and wisdom—residing within the chamber of your heart. Let the image be as clear as you are able to make it.

Be aware of the perfect clarity of this being. Let your heart be filled with the love he or she radiates.

Now imagine this divine being growing in size, reaching out to fill the boundary of your own body, your own skin. Experience love and wisdom permeating your entire body. Rest in this awareness for a few moments.

As you continue breathing, let the expansion continue, and let your own edges move outward so that you grow in size together with the holy one.

Grow until you fill the room . . . the building . . . the neighborhood . . . the city or county in which you are right now. Grow until you are as large as the state . . . the continent . . . the Earth. Continue expanding until you fill the solar system . . . the galaxy . . . the universe.

Now observe, within your skin, countless stars and endless empty space. Take note of a million worlds, each with its own life forms and consciousnesses. Look toward the world from which you came; regard its smallness and its rich abundance of life; embrace it all just as it is.

Observe the daily course of life on this planet. Look toward what was your own life . . . and toward others'. Watch as long and as many as you like in an infinite instant of time. From here you can see your own birth and death, your parents and grandparents and the dramas of their lives; from here you can watch the rise and fall of civilizations; from here you can visit each individual being and share their joys and sorrows. Feel the expansion of your perspective, the growth of wisdom and compassion.

From wisdom regard your place of birth, the planet Earth. In compassion regard the one who is called yourself.

Now, gently, prepare for your return. Allow your boundaries to contract ever so slightly . . . then a little more. Shrinking, shrinking, come back through distant galaxies, back through the great clouds of space, back through stars and black holes, touching all, distracted by none, your direction the return to your own self.

Return to your native solar system; come back to the size of Earth's orbit. Continue growing smaller until you embrace only Earth herself within your skin. Returning, returning, come back through clouds and mists, mountains and oceans, cities and forests. Come back, ever shrinking, until you reach the one called you, the body from which you started.

Gently, gently settle your edges to match the skin of your self. Gently *begin to note the activities of the body again, the beat of the heart, the rush of blood, the swoosh of breath.*

Residing again within human form, allow yourself to imagine that the one who is holy continues to become smaller, smaller, while your skin remains the same. Let that wide space of love and knowing become ever more concentrated until it is, again, a tiny being about the size of your thumb, residing in the chamber of your heart.

When you are ready, feel your way fully back into the body. Slowly open your eyes; with small movements of your body, slowly begin to return to your present life, as a human being who is fully engaged upon this Earth.

If you find yourself weeping on your return from the infinite, recognize now the supreme gift of Jesus, of Buddha, of all the holy ones who came back to be with us. From your vast home, come home broken-hearted to your own people, to your own life.[18]

7

What Do You Do?

> Question: What do you do when you get to the top of a hundred-foot pole?
> Answer: Take one step forward.
> —FROM CASE 46 OF *The Gateless Barrier*

Sit Down

In Sanskrit there is a word, "*jhana,*" that means "a state of bliss." The concept came to China and was named *chan,* then to Japan and named *zen.* The word *zazen,* or sitting meditation, means to sit down with others in this wonderful state. Zazen has no purpose other than itself.

To practice zazen is to be present with the breath, to let its ebb and flow sink into your awareness, into your body, to be present with rising and falling breath, and rising and falling thoughts, rather than trying to escape from either. Not to try to escape is essential. There is nothing in you, your body or mind, that you have any reason to run away from.

This is true even if you have committed acts that you (or others) regard as terrible or unforgivable. To be human encompasses everything. To run away from your past, or your thoughts, is to refuse to be human.

To sit down, to face ourselves, is to let in something that will strengthen us, that will begin to create the space inside that has the possibility and the power to mend. It is to heal ourselves by accepting ourselves. Even though zazen has no purpose except our being present, these things happen.

It's not that the way we start out in zazen is by accepting ourselves. Rather, we start out simply by sitting down, listening to that voice criticizing over and over again. Eventually, gradually, we become patient with that voice, or with the being who is subjected to the criticism, or perhaps with both at once. Since both of them are us, we thus have begun to accept ourselves.

And then certain outward signs—calmness, friendliness, equanimity—begin to develop. These are evidence that something inside is becoming clearer, more transparent: our "true nature" is shining through.

What is this true nature? It is the place where we all are one, where everything happens as it should, the place of perfect love, the opening of the heart.

Zazen is simply being present with our breath, letting its ebb and flow sink into our awareness; we become attuned to the rhythms of our own breathing and our own heartbeats.

We also become attuned to the rhythms of our own minds. Just as the skin secretes perspiration, so the mind secretes thoughts. In zazen, what we do with these naturally arising thoughts is release them. When we follow a particularly compelling thought, then notice that we've followed it, we release it and return to our breath. Thus we become very well acquainted with our thoughts, feelings, and desires—without judging them and without changing them.

To do this—to be present with ourselves without trying to fix ourselves—is a remarkable and unusual activity. Even a brief period in which we stay present (rather than daydreaming or criticizing) is transformative. It expands; it leads to the possibility of going through daily life without escaping or complaining. It leads to a quietness, an imperturbability, an equanimity. After you've sat zazen awhile, you can simply get into the upright sitting posture and, through habit, distressed thoughts and moods will start to ease up.

A big wind will create great waves on a shallow lake but only small ones on a deep lake. In the same way, the disturbances of everyday life create less disruption in a life supported and deepened by the practice of sitting meditation.

When you begin this practice, you may first go deeper into distress; but over time, sitting meditation brings a depth that helps you face that distress—and its causes.

To sit down with the breath is to invite, to allow, to welcome the support of the entire universe, to receive the blessing of the One that stands behind all existence, and to simultaneously offer that blessing to all beings.

This happens with each breath, whether you are aware of it or not.

Just Stand Up

Zen students, like everyone, often complain about their lives. Katagiri Roshi would listen patiently to his students, but his fundamental recommendation was simple. "Stand up in your life," he would tell us. "Just stand up."

To be awake is to receive all of life as the colors of the rainbow—all life's beauty, all suffering, everything. This is where we are headed, this openness, this welcoming of whatever comes to us.

But it's not always where we are right now. So if you can't receive everything that comes to you with joy, then you can just stand up. Then you take responsibility for living this day. You stand up in each moment, with the support of the earth and of your own spine; you breathe your own breath and think your own thoughts.

When you stand up, you stay present with the blaming mind as well as the aching bones. Whether you're facing physical pain, interpersonal problems, economic difficulties, or your own faults, you stay present without running away.

If you cannot live this day well, then you just live it however you can.

Wrestle with God

We are accustomed to struggling with things smaller than ourselves, and winning; but the object is to struggle with things greater than ourselves, and to lose.
—Ranier Maria Rilke, "Der Schauende"
or "The Man Watching"

When I was a child, I learned the story of Jacob wrestling with the angel. He wrestled all night. He neither won nor lost, but in the morning he was given a new name and a limp. Afterward, he honored that site as the place where he met God.[19]

To wrestle with God is to undertake the most difficult of all things. It's so much easier just to give in, to say, "Thy will be done," to let go of large matters and just tend to your own business.

But the truth is, you *can't* always leave it alone. There are times when you cannot pretend that you accept what God is doing—whether in your personal life or in international affairs. Accepting your life does not mean pretending you accept it; being spiritual does not mean being a doormat even for the divine. Being spiritual means being responsible for your life, and responsibility for your life means that when you have a complaint, you will take it to the source.

So you seek out God, and you admit that you want something.

Whether it's the end of racism or the healing of your own cancer, you put forth your agenda without shame or embarrassment. You address God. Whether you use some other name or image does not matter; but if you do not personify God, you will have to encounter that mystery even more directly. Such a meeting is intimate and filled with energy.

You can say anything to God, and you can say it as often and as vehemently as you need. You do not have to quit until you are satisfied. You do have to give respect. You will receive it.

This is wrestling with God. I've made it sound rational and reasonable, but in fact it's no such thing. You sought out God, but there are times when you see nothing, know nothing, and are not sure whether your opponent is demon, human, or divine. You may be terrified; you may be exhausted. Like Jacob, you may wrestle all night, or through half your life. In the end, if you stay with it, if you do not give in and do not give up, you may have the good fortune to be wounded by God.

To wrestle with God is to re-create your self.

To wrestle with God gives life. Though it is sometimes exhausting, the struggle ultimately does not tear you down. It tests you; it brings you more fully into yourself. Even when you think you are dying, you have a glimmer of understanding that what's dying is a smaller version of yourself. And so you find yourself willing.

During that long night, the most difficult and persistent question is often "Who is this who wrestles with me?" Doubt over this question can bring you to despair. Or hope and despair may alternate—perhaps every thirty seconds.

Yet even then, there is an answer: Treat your opponent as God. Because God is always there.

The Scripture does not record that Jacob—renamed Israel—ever complained about his limp.

Practice

"You should make writing your practice," Katagiri Roshi said to Natalie Goldberg.
"Why?" she asked.
"Because you like it," came the answer.
She puzzled for a bit. Then she asked, "Do you like to do zazen?"
"Yes," he said.
—NATALIE GOLDBERG, *WRITING DOWN THE BONES*

People think of practice as something done for a purpose, as a way to get ready for an event such as a show or a game. But the word "practice" actually means just doing something, over and over again, with attention. This could apply to flute practice, football practice, martial arts practice, or anything. The idea that practice isn't the real thing—that it's just a rehearsal for the real thing—is an unnecessary addition.

We tend to think of a spiritual practice as something we do for a purpose: to make us better, wiser, more patient, more compassionate, or even more powerful. We expect it to be difficult and not particularly pleasant. We think that what is good for us must (like medicine) taste bad unless it is sugar-coated. And we either disdain the sugar coating for diluting the medicine or seek it eagerly.

But in truth, what we like is good for us. To throw ourselves wholeheartedly into what makes us happy, what makes us feel most alive, makes us more happy, more alive.

The essential meaning of a spiritual practice is something you can and will continue to do, long enough and attentively enough that you get to know yourself through your relationship to it. Spiritual practice carries you into knowing yourself in detail—your quirks and stubbornnesses and virtues. It also carries you into your larger self (called true nature by Buddhists, called God by some others), into something vast and alive and joyful, into the source of everything beyond words. Practice takes you not into intellectual knowledge but into experience itself. And in practice you become able to tolerate and even embrace all those maddening idiosyncrasies of your small self.

So, a suitable practice is something that you like; it is something you can do, and keep doing, for the rest of your life; it is something that is beneficial rather than harmful to you and others.

It's convenient if your spiritual practice doesn't cost money; it's best by far if it's something you can share with others. Beyond this, though, don't worry too much about what that practice is.

Sometimes you may choose something as practice that really doesn't work—or sometimes it works for a while, then no longer works. Sometimes it needs to be shifted, often just slightly. Knowing whether to make an adjustment, to stay with what you're doing, or to take up something new is a practice in itself, requiring very close attention to your inner direction. Advice can be helpful at such a time, especially advice from someone who knows you well, or from a wise teacher, or (preferably) from someone who is both.

But even (and especially) when you are in such an uncertain state, continue with your practice. It will care for you when you allow it. And the results of staying with your practice (until and unless it transforms itself into something else) are like the difference between a fifty-year marriage and a lifetime of one-night stands.

If we feel guilty about doing things we like, this can hinder our practice.

For years I denied myself the things that most attracted me—including study with a deeply insightful spiritual teacher who lived in my city—because I believed that I should spend all of my time in political activism. Had I followed my genuine longing, I might have been able to be a more effective activist as well as being happier. Instead I spent another five years searching for my path while simultaneously stopping myself.

Self-denial in itself is not a useful practice. The original and appropriate use of self-denial is this: to give up anything that stands in the way of your deepest, most central desire.

This desire has been given many names: self-realization, calling, being true to yourself, even "doing your own thing." My own favorite names are "homesickness for God" and "the longing to return to your own true nature."

There is another basic pitfall: if we think doing something we like means that practice should always be easy or fun, we will never deeply enter our practice—*or* our life. The thing that in small doses was delightful, nourishing, and comforting begins to change shape when we take it up seriously. When we invite it to become part of our lives, it begins to show us parts of ourselves that we might rather keep hidden. This can become frightening or very uncomfortable.

But something wonderful waits for us just on the other side of the discomfort: ourselves. Every time we make it through another layer of discomfort (each one probably more difficult than the last) we have more strength, more vitality, more of ourselves.

Practicing with what you like is inviting life itself into you.

And yet you don't have to find the perfect, custom-made practice before you can start. If you spend your life looking for the perfect practice, you are spending it in the practice of dissatisfaction.

If you are digging a well, and you keep digging in the same place, eventually you'll reach water. But if you keep looking around for a better place, you may end up with a bunch of holes and no water. Looking first for a place that's not solid granite is probably a good idea, but once you've found it, dig!

Want

"I want" has two interpretations. One is called in Buddhism "the inmost request," meaning the deepest desire of your nature: the desire to return home, to be free from illusion, to be full of joy, to realize your connection with all of creation.

The other "I want" is everyday desire, and often corresponds to addictions, escape, avoidance—all the things that come up in us because the inmost request brings with it some heavy demands.

Freedom brings responsibility; sometimes it feels like too much and we would rather just watch TV. Insight reveals to us some things that we would rather not know; and each of us has our own collection of things we're willing to know and other things we'd like to ignore or deny.

But once we've acknowledged our inmost request, it does not so easily leave us alone. There can be a long period of discomfort before any satisfaction comes. During that time, we learn to listen within, to trust our inner guidance, again and again and again. We learn to forgive ourselves for the thousand blunders we make each day. We learn to distinguish between selfishness and the inner voice.

This voice urges some of us to engage in active lives, immersed in the doings of civilization, politics, and society. It leads others to family life, with relationship at the center. Still others are drawn directly to the internal search for liberation. All these paths lead to the same destination.

Following the inmost request brings us face to face with the whole thing: life, God, angels, ourselves, each other. The path that looks like sitting quietly in a monastery leads to the same place as the one that looks like giving your life away as a saint or hero.

The journey in is the journey home, and when we arrive home all the others come to meet us.

Ask the Question

Fifteen of us had been talking for some time about a fairy tale and its meaning for human life. "We're talking around the center," said Evangeline, "making circles around it rather than going straight to it."

I asked her, "How do you go directly to the center?"

She answered: "When you're going to sleep at night, think that you will die before you wake, and go to sleep anyway."

I felt a piercing, a shattering. The power of the reply shot through me, lightning from the inside. And though the room was full of people, I felt her instruction was mine alone.

Her answer was a practice: "Do this." Trying to follow it kept me wide awake that whole night and disturbed my sleep for many more. It changed something in me at a level too deep to describe; I thought of it as altering the very molecular structure of the cells of my body.

There is such a thing as the right question. It leaps up from within; it recognizes the moment and seizes it.

And then, when the answer comes, you have to let it in. Like a scalpel, it can cut away what is no longer needed. It can let light into closed up places, can open the tomb.

Take Up Your Life

When the question comes, when the time is right, you have to ask. Listen carefully to the answer.

Ask for Help

We sought through prayer and meditation to improve our conscious contact with God as we understood God, praying only for knowledge of God's will and the power to carry it out.

—ALCOHOLICS ANONYMOUS, ELEVENTH STEP

Sometimes we think that we never ought to pray for tangible or practical things. At other times, we reject this idea as one rooted in shame; we acknowledge that wants and needs are natural, and we decide that the best approach is to freely ask for things.

Some spiritual teachers suggest that when we have a request, we ask wholeheartedly and then entirely let it go, leaving its disposal entirely at God's will.

Others encourage us to ask again and again until we receive a definitive answer, or even until we receive the answer we seek.

Others say that before we even ask we are answered and therefore the appropriate way to pray is to give thanks for the blessing granted and to expect its fruition.

Still others tell us not to ask for anything at all but to accept whatever is given to us with joy and gratitude.

All of these approaches are correct.

Each is an honest and human way to relate to what lies far beyond us. As long as demands, orders, and assumptions are left behind, we may fruitfully enter any of these paths of prayer.

Take Up Your Life

As long as our choice of path is based not on how to best manipulate the deep powers but on an honest relationship, we may proceed safely. As long as we remember our authentic place in the universe—that we are neither outsider nor its center—we can ask for help in any way we wish.

Enter the Maze

From time to time, it appears for a moment: as we sit quietly, or walk in a snowstorm, or exert every muscle in work, or look into another's eyes, the opening comes. Suddenly we are free. Like a flash it happens—and then we notice it, want it to stay. In our wanting, the moment disappears; by the next breath it is gone. Only its memory remains.

It is our wish to hold the moment that sends it away. Yet there is no point in trying not to want. Rather, allow the process—the opening, the recognition, the clinging, the loss and regret. We can't go back to the moment, and every attempt to do so delays the possibility of the next such opening.

Each precious moment gives birth to a memory. The memory both nourishes us and traps us. To wish it otherwise is to wish for ultimate freedom, to insist on enlightenment NOW.

Go ahead and wish. Make every effort not to wish. Do both at the same time. Laugh at how impossible it is, how silly you are for even trying. Now try again. This is the maze called life.

Duty

A man was about to jump off a bridge. Just as he was beginning his leap, someone came by and grabbed him. His rescuer, though still holding tightly to him, was pulled off balance until he too dangled precariously off the bridge. A third man came by and grabbed him, and after a bit of teetering was able to pull both men back onto the bridge.

When they were all back to safety, a passerby asked the first rescuer, "Why didn't you just let go?"

He said, "If I had let go, it wouldn't have been worth living."

It's more important to be connected with each other than to be individually alive. That man knew it. He knew it so vividly that there was no question about what to do.

Most of us don't know it so vividly. It's too easy to go to sleep. It's too easy to forget about connection unless your own connection to the rest is being challenged or attacked. And even then there are plenty of sedatives around.

When our minds remember the necessity of connection, but we don't yet feel it with our whole bodies, that is also called duty. When we respond to a situation without worrying about how it will impact our own life (even our spiritual life), that is called duty.

Duty has been confused with both guilt and shame though it has nothing to do with either. Rather, it is the memory of our connection with each other. It is a promise to keep even when that connection no longer actively lives and breathes in our awareness.

If there were abundance, if there were love, if there were *enough*, duty would not be needed. Duty comes into play when love and joy have worn themselves thin, but we still remember what must be done. Duty keeps the family fed, clothed, and bathed; it cannot give them more. Duty smells like old sawdust, looks like a worn-out woman—thin and tired, with uncared-for hair and too many children. Duty has a feel of poverty about it.

Duty, at best, stands in for love. It remembers when the heart is tired.

When duty comes with resentment, it eats away the insides. The heart becomes a chunk of gravel, a black hard rock of tar; the bones are eaten by acid and the muscles wither; the breath atrophies to a mere whisper instead of a full wind.

I have seen people burn themselves out in duty, doing the right thing despite the pressing need for a good night's sleep. Yet having burned off what looked like self—what was in fact an armor—they went beyond the resentment, came back new and more alive, more awake, more here.

This is what we must remember: that duty has to do with love. To go on when you don't want to, to give when you have nothing more to give, is to stay connected.

And the gift, ultimately, comes from the whole. When you stay connected in this way, you become a channel for the forces of life. To be such a channel is to be washed by life yourself, to be cleansed as though a stream is rushing through you.

The need that presents itself in each moment is life's offering *to you*. It is exactly what your life has brought you as your task, right now. To turn away from it is to turn away from your own life.

Take Up Your Life

Still, that is not the reason to hold to duty. The reason is—and always has been—that you remember your connection with all people and all living things. You hold to duty because *you* are alive, and to be alive is to be one with all.

Duty has gone out of public favor, eclipsed by "following your bliss." Yet duty is not *against* following your bliss; rather, it educates that following, turns it from childish whim or adolescent rebellion to the searching, hard work of the adult.

In hard times, when we do not feel connected with each other, we can fall back on duty; we can use our minds to regenerate what our hearts have temporarily forgotten. We can think: What does the community need? What does the future require? What will best care for the whole Earth? What is my place in all of this? Then bliss informs duty.

If we will reclaim duty, if we accept the breaking, accept the pain, accept responsibility—if we maybe even give up some of that glorified personal freedom—then at the end we will know our place in the world. At the end we will have ourselves and each other.

A Great Work

I do not know whether there is such a thing as a life without a calling or only a life without a calling named. It may be that for some, the work of a lifetime is simply to do what comes to hand. Indeed, that is praised as the spiritual way to live: whatever is needed in this moment, that is the right thing to do now. "When hungry, eat; when tired, sleep."

The problem arises when "whatever is needed" appears as something that happens on the scale of a lifetime or more—a great work.

To have a calling is to have something particular you're supposed to do, something bigger than you, a responsibility to the world or to your people or to God. And that means you eventually *have* to do it. You can avoid it for years, but there will be a restless grumbling inside of you. You'll never be quite satisfied, even though you may be well fed.

If you let that grumbling guide you as it's supposed to do, you will be signing up for the kind of dissatisfaction shared by artists and poets. And yet you must sign up for it, for it is exactly what you need to be whole. And somehow you must find a way to support your body and life.

Whatever way you find to do this, it's important not to be swept away by the kind of hopelessness in which a weekend (or a week's salary) disappears into your struggle to escape the thought that you're not doing your work yet. No. Instead, keep yourself going, either by noticing the minute ways in which you actually already are doing it or by actively getting ready to do it in some way. Then, when the opportunity appears—whether to begin, to continue, or to deepen your work—you'll be able to step forward into it.

When you take up a calling, you are taking up something specific. This is true even if your work appears to be something totally spiritual or esoteric. You are taking up something that belongs uniquely to you, that is as particular as your own fingerprints.

This means that you are getting involved with your ego, your personality, your self. Looking for the universal, the beyond, the ecstatic, the holy, you are drawn irretrievably into that in you which is particular, present, and mundane.

Your work is designed specifically for the particular person you are, the one who was born to certain parents and has a particular history and memory and self-awareness. When you take on a calling, you accept this individuality: you accept roots in the world.

This work, your work, is designed to lead you through your individual self to wholeness. This wholeness is also the connection with all beings. It can lead you beyond your individual self, but only if you go fully into it in all its particulars.

Your work is your connection with the whole, often in some very literal way. Perhaps you cook food, which nourishes other human beings; perhaps you have entered politics and grapple with decisions that shape human lives.

To really engage in a great work involves you in mortality. You may fail; you may die; the work may die. Yet in order to really live you have to take it up. Whatever the task is, large or small, you have to take it up, or you will pass your life rather than live it.

Some religions, and some sects and branches, are organized around a wish to escape this world, this vale of tears with its distractions and temptations, for the place where everything is divine. Others delight in the world, finding divinity everywhere *right here* in spite of the apparent contradictions. Then there are those that exist within both spaces at once.

When we hold work in a certain way, we are in both these spaces at once. Coming from the other world, the place of unity, we greet the world of diversity without discrimination. We enter the multitude of things and ideas without considering them inferior or illusive or distracting. We do not have a goal that is somewhere else; nor do we attempt to not have a goal. Rather, our goal is right here in this world. Staying with this goal, we are in the world of unity and bliss. Then, simultaneously, we have life here on Earth and life here in the awakened state.

To take up a calling is to get engaged in detail, in pettiness; to sometimes lose the grand design, to chance losing the forest for the trees. You accept responsibility for having an impact in this life. You become willing to take on all the parts of it, pleasant and unpleasant; you find people to work with, whether you like them or not; you deal with money, ego, and desire; you compromise and sometimes refuse to compromise; you are willing to be a public figure, or

Take Up Your Life

not, as required; you put yourself out there in some way and take the chance of failing.

And if you haven't found your work yet, if you can hear it calling vaguely but not specifically, it's no problem. For the moment, do something that is needed in the world. Whether paid or unpaid, there is real work to do: work that can partially satisfy the need for your own work and more than partially satisfy the need to serve.

If you take up a work and pour yourself into it, the power of love and service will flow through you and teach you, shape you and use you and transform you. And as you continue, you will become stronger and also clearer about the nature of your particular work. Or you will be fully satisfied and can remain exactly where you are.

So don't waste your time searching for the answer. When it is time, you won't be able to miss it.

Invitation

Following the Inner Guide

Sit or stand in the middle of an open space—such as a large carpeted room or a private grassy area outdoors—with bare feet and loose comfortable clothing.

Bring your attention to your skin: notice the air contacting it, the feel of your clothes against it, the contact of your hair. Be aware of its roughness or smoothness, its temperature and texture, all the qualities that belong to your skin. Get acquainted with the nature of skin.

Now, in the same way, explore muscle. As you breathe in and out, notice the movement of muscles in that motion. Notice the muscles lying under every inch of skin. Discover where tension and relaxation lie. Become friends with the quality of muscle.

Next, bring your attention to your skeleton. Investigate all the bones, their connections, the spaces between them. Long bones and short ones, curved and straight, simple and complex—get acquainted with the bony structure that supports your whole body.

Then focus in on your spine. Give attention to this curved and flexible stack of vertebrae. Notice the spaces between the bones, the openness of the disks that cushion its moves, its ability to flex, to twist, and to hold your body upright. Consider the channel it makes for the nervous system to travel through, reaching throughout your body.

Now move into the space just in front of your spine, an inch or two deep, stretching the entire length of the spine. Feel energy moving up and down it as you breathe. Think to yourself that this is the core of your body. Notice its relation to all the other layers of your self. Breathe a few breaths with this deep and living space.

In a few moments, a movement will arise from your core. Breathing, waiting, be attentive and recognize its direction when it comes. Then gently allow your body to move, however it is drawn to move. (If after a few more patient breaths you have not recognized a direction, move your torso either left or right. Notice whether the movement feels comfortable or alien. If it feels unnatural, you will probably have a "Not that, this" feeling. Follow the "this" now.) The movement from the core will feel natural, comfortable, native to you.

Continue to follow the movements that come naturally, moment by moment, for several minutes. These movements may evolve into a kind of play, or dance, or discovery; they may settle into stillness briefly or at length. Stay with the movements, allowing them to arise and fall in their own natural rhythm. This is your body's talk; listen to it fully.

Do this for as long as you like. Then come to stillness and attend to your body, your mind, and your emotions; note what follows this intense presence with yourself.

Suggestions

If you have trouble getting started, music probably will help you begin to move. Use music that you like. Later you can try again without music. More focused attention is required when you don't have an outside rhythm to follow, so the silent mode may be more intense.

If emotions come up, don't stop moving. Instead, notice where you feel them in the body and whether they want to express themselves through movement.

You may do this with a group as well. Just don't worry about either looking silly (you will!) or doing it "right."

If you like, set a specific length of time for this practice, and don't stop until the time is up.

Taking a class with a movement teacher or dance therapist can be enormously helpful if you have difficulty with this exercise—*or* if you find it delightful and want guidance in carrying it further.

The basic guidelines for this meditation are:

- Pay attention.

- Follow your guidance.

- Stay with it.

8

The Taste of Freedom

> To deny the reality of things is to miss their reality. To assert the emptiness of things is to miss their reality.
> The more you talk and think about it, the further astray you wander from the truth. Stop talking and thinking, and there is nothing you will not be able to know. To return to the root is to find the meaning.
> —SENG-TS'AN, SIXTH-CENTURY ZEN MASTER,
> *THE HSIN HSIN MING*
>
> Trees and grasses, wall and fence expound and exalt the dharma for the sake of ordinary people, sages, and all living beings. Ordinary people, sages, and all living beings in turn preach and exalt the dharma for the sake of trees, grasses, wall, and fence. . . . When even just one person, at one time, sits in zazen . . . they are performing the eternal and ceaseless work of guiding beings to enlightenment.
> —DOGEN, *JIJUYU ZAMMAI*
> *(SELF-FULFILLING SAMADHI)*

What Cannot Be Named

The unknown and the mysterious belong in this world. Only then is life whole.
—CARL JUNG, *MEMORIES, DREAMS, REFLECTIONS*

Religion is not a way to make your life work better or to get what you want. Religion is a way to invite something larger than yourself into your life.

Religion has exactly to do with *not* being in control, with being small in the face of something larger—something we can touch but cannot truly name.

We often think of this unnameable energy as different from ourselves and separate from our ordinary life. We build cathedrals to it; upon meeting it we are naturally moved to silence, to a bow, to whatever is our own most powerful gesture of respect.

That something we refer to as God. Or Goddess, Allah, Great Spirit, Higher Power, The Mystery, the universe, the Infinite, the Unknowable—we have many names for what cannot be named.

There is a difference between these names and those that are personified: Jesus, Shiva, Kwan Yin, Avalokitesvara, Eshun, White Buffalo Woman. These beings each represent a specific quality or have a particular story. (Of course, God often is personified, which creates considerable confusion, and Goddess is personified more often than not; still, the terms imply the quality of the beyond, not a person.)

Probably the best way to talk about this something is found in Judaism. The name of God is YHVH, Yod Hay Vav Hay—four Hebrew letters, each with a meaning, combined in a way that cannot be pronounced, and so holy that if it is written down, that writing must be forever guarded as a sacred object. Some Christians have attempted to make this a name, pronounced "Jehovah" or "Yahweh," but by doing so they lose the whole meaning of the name that cannot be named.

And it is found everywhere. "Thusness," says the Song of the Jewel Mirror Awareness (a ninth-century Buddhist scripture), is something that is intimately communicated. "Turning away and touching are both wrong, for it is like a mass of fire." It cannot be spoken or written, given or conveyed by ordinary means. The *Tao te Ching* expresses this eloquently: "The Way that can be named is not the eternal Way; the Name that can be named is not the eternal Name."

Though this something can neither be named nor communicated, the natural response to meeting it is to offer it to others. Descriptions, structures, rules, definitions—all the paraphernalia of religion—arise from the human effort to share something that is beyond our capacity to tell. And so a religion is born, whenever another way is found to "look on the face of God and live."

Give Thanks

Innumerable labors have brought us this food
We should know how it comes to us
As we receive this offering, we should consider
Whether our virtue and practice deserve it. . . .
—CHANT BEFORE MEALS, SOTO ZEN TRADITION

Another part of religion is about gratitude—creating a space to express our response to the Mystery.

The lines just quoted are a small part of the traditional meal chant from Zen Buddhist monasteries, and they guide us toward the possibility of gratitude.

There is no way that our virtue and practice can *deserve* the food we eat. Even if we cultivate the soil, sow the seed, water and weed, harvest, and cook and serve the meal, the growth from seed to life-giving fruit is still a gift from the bountiful nature of the universe. When we consider our relationship to the natural world, we must notice there is no way to earn our daily bread. It is always a gift.

It is good to remember this about our lives: they are given to us.

Givenness as a quality of life naturally calls forth a response. The response is gratitude, and gratitude is heaven. Gratitude is the presence of God.

When you open yourself to this natural response, it changes everything. Gratitude opens *you* up. It helps you to grow lighter and more flexible. It makes it possible to look outside your small shell and actually recognize what is there.

Giving thanks, you begin to soften the boundaries you had set up to keep the world away. You make windows and, finally, doors in your protective wall. Giving thanks, you become more and more accessible to the people and events of your life. And they become more accessible to you.

And when you can find nothing in your life that even remotely inspires gratitude—when the Mystery remains hidden and the numinous does not shine through, when sorrow and injustice are everywhere—that is when the practice of giving thanks has the most to offer.

However difficult it may be, when you give thanks you are no longer alone. When you give thanks, you begin to find your place in the world. When you give thanks, you become part of the universe rather than its center. Here, in gratitude, you can enter your community; here you can meet the whole world.

Birth and Death

A breath enters the body, moves down into the lungs, becomes an expansion of the diaphragm and a softening of the belly—then leaves the body and returns to the vastness of the atmosphere. Breath takes on the form of the human being doing the breathing and then is released again into union with all air.

There is something about this that is like birth and death: we take on individual form; we return to the whole.

In the earliest stories of Buddha and his disciples, the moment of awakening is described again and again as the realization of this truth: "All that is subject to arising is subject to cessation."

It is good for us to notice that we will come to an end. Contemplating ourselves as ephemeral, like the breath entering and leaving, like the waves washing upon the shore, helps loosen our attachment to the past and to the future. It helps us to let go, to be like leaves on the wind, to open the fist that clenches.

We all will die. Yet everything we know about after death comes from hearsay.

Something continues after death, but what is it really?

There is someone in me who thinks and interprets, who looks

out at the world and at each experience, who is in essence the same now at age forty-six as she was at age twelve, or even at three. This someone, called "self" or "ego" or "I," is actually a function: it receives stimuli from the senses and assigns meaning to what is received. Imagining that this same receiving-and-interpreting experience will continue after death requires a large stretch of the imagination.

What is this, this faculty of taking in, interpreting, making decisions, directing actions? We give it a name—the self—but what exactly is it? Despite all that psychology, sociology, and genetics have offered us, the truth is we don't know what the self is.

There is an image, from Buddhism, that the passage of life from one human body to the next is like the passing of a flame from one candle to another. Something is passed on, but it's hard to say what.

Bringing us into birth, this flame creates the forms and structures that limit us: not just each particular body but also the family, country, social and economic circumstances, and genetic and psychological factors. And like fire, like a breath, it also brings in everything that gives us joy and makes life worth living.

Out of this paradox, our self is born, only to die again when its time comes, to pass its fire to the next waiting candle.

Take Up Your Life

This self is both a treasure and a heavy burden. To love flowers, to treasure the scent of the ocean, to delight in silly play or in earnest discussion—the details of what makes *this* life worthwhile belong to the self. Here also dwell the details that cause us pain: self-doubt, resentment, cynicism, loneliness.

The more lightly we hold that self, the less importance we place on it, the freer and easier our lives become.

Think how much easier it is to drive a compact car than a large truck. If we cling tightly to our particular delights, we need something like a truck to carry all the pieces of our lives; but if we can relax and let go of details, our lives become freer, simpler, as easy to handle as a small car.

And yet, you can't *just* let go of all your personal details. First you have to know that releasing your treasures means something more than just not having them. You have to be willing to find out that the whole universe supports you at every moment; you have to have an opening large enough for love to come in. Only then can you find freedom in letting go the details of personality.

In fact, only then is it *possible* to let them go.

If you lack the security of that boundless support, you may try to suppress your individuality in an effort to let go. When you do this, you find that you are now holding on in two places instead of one. It is only within the safety of the infinite, the support of God's love, that the hard shell of self can gradually soften and relax.

The Voice of Recognition

There was a Zen monk who, after years of study and practice, despaired of ever reaching enlightenment. With his teacher's permission, he gave up his meditation practice and instead served meals to the monks.

After eight years of kitchen work, he became enlightened.

He went to his teacher, who acknowledged that he had awakened at last.

The teacher in this story knew that the student had the capacity to awaken and that eight years of despair, or twenty, or a hundred, would lead him there. The teacher had the space to wait; his heart was large and he knew compassion. And, when the student was ready, he was there to say yes.

This is an essential quality of a teacher: the ability to offer recognition.

When we haven't found an awakened teacher to do this for us, we can do it for each other.

We must be willing to hear the truth, no matter who speaks it. And we must be willing to tell the truth, when the need is there.

Let God appear; let enlightenment speak. Don't be embarrassed to offer that touch to someone whose time has come, who asks you for acknowledgment. Don't look for the moment, but if it appears, don't turn away from the challenge.

To allow Truth to speak through you is to widen the channel within yourself, forever.

Right There

The sound that issues from the striking of emptiness is an endless and wondrous voice that resounds before and after the fall of the hammer.
—Dogen, *Jijuyu Zammai* (Self-Fulfilling Samadhi)

The strength to live and be lived: joy.
—Dainin Katagiri

There is a sense of being rung like a bell. Permeating, resounding, alive and boundless, reality echoes in the deep places of our being. Skin and flesh are of little substance in comparison, resting lightly on this truth: that we are one, are essence, are lived by all beings. We have no separate existence but instead the breath of all life, the vibrant resonance of the bell. Joy consists of allowing this truth, of knowing that we are lived.

Whether you name as One that which breathes you and beats your heart, or whether you refuse even that small illusion of separation, there it is. To doubt is to turn away from it. To doubt is to stifle the breath, to dampen the sound of the bell, to refuse to be lit by the fire. To doubt is to try to go it alone.

The vast space is right there, right behind each breath, a brilliant shadow of each cell of our bodies, a brilliant echo of each molecule of air. It can be soft and gentle, or dazzling, shattering, more than we can handle. It is always there.

Take Up Your Life

The light shines through, lives deep inside the core of being. We are supported by all living things, *lived by* all beings.

This is a door, waiting for each of us to pass through it. After entering it, it is never possible to go back again. Going through it, you know that it is possible to live, no matter what. You know that escape is not necessary. Somewhere deep inside you, you know wholeness.

Having passed through this doorway, you take up residence in a landscape filled with color and life. You tap into the vastness, the opening, the source, the Source. You become—and you remain—fully human, fully present with the beauty and tragedy of human life.

The sound of the bell resonates before and after the fall of the hammer, in every bone and tissue of the body, in every molecule of air, in every encounter.

What Do You Do?

And still the question remains, in each moment, a hundred times each day: "What do I do?"

Keep on going. As well as you can, take up your life; embrace your life. Hold in your heart all those you meet. Forgive yourself again and again. Give thanks. Open to the holy.

You do not need to control your life; just live it. You do not need to control other people; just meet them. You do not need to control yourself; just be who you are. You have this ability; you have this freedom.

Something beyond, something powerful and generous is in charge. It shapes your life. It is the strongest force inside every human heart and mind.

Whatever the struggles of your life—ideas, politics, relationships—as you engage more fully, you become ever more present with this force.

Mother Theresa was a nun in Calcutta when something moved her. She went into the street and lived with the poor people, and her life opened up. We don't know how hungry she got before the miracle of love happened, but we know the results.

Joanna Macy worked and wrote about nuclear danger, about despair and empowerment; she searched for how to live in this world; she gave what she had. Now she has taken up, as a personal responsibility, the problem of long-term protection of nuclear wastes, simply because somebody has to do it.

Morris Dees directs the Southern Poverty Law Center on the front lines against racism and intolerance in America. He risks his life—and he makes a difference.

Peace Pilgrim looked like an ordinary housewife back in the 1950s. For some reason she made a vow to walk for peace, and walked across America for the rest of her life. She walked quietly, lived quietly, and wrote a few pamphlets on what she believed. When last seen there was nothing ordinary about her at all.

We must each make our own choice between hope and despair. And sometimes you will have to live with despair before hope becomes possible. Sometimes you must go all the way into despair before you can give it up, give up on it. After this, when despair has become impossible, then hope is much more than merely possible—it is fully present. The hope that arises after the end of despair is a hope that is fully alive, unimaginably vast and deep, completely nourishing.

Life half asleep is not worth living. Choose clarity, choose love. Accept difficulty, stay with it, stay with yourself, stay with what is larger than you. There is nothing more precious than such a life.

Invitation

Take some time to cultivate gratitude in your life.

Gratitude: Part I

Begin by giving thanks for what you have in general, even if you don't know whom you're thanking.

Now, internally, thank every person who's done something you can recognize as helpful. Thank your parents for giving you life. Thank the last person who cheered you up or made you laugh. Thank the last person who helped you learn a difficult lesson. Thank them silently, internally, or speak your thanks aloud to them.

Then thank the food you eat for supporting your life. If it tastes good, thank it again, and thank the cook. Thank the vehicles that transport you, the workers who made them, those who sold them, the earth that produced the metals, the companies that refined and delivered the fuel—and so on.

Thank the wind and sky and sun and rain for the weather when you like it; and when you don't, thank the trees and builders who created your shelter.

When your car breaks down, thank whoever repairs it or whoever taught you the skills to do it yourself. Thank the parts shop, and the telephone, and whatever means of transportation you use meanwhile, however inconvenient. If you have to walk, be thankful for shoes, sidewalks or paths, and healthy legs. If you can't walk, be thankful for the transportation you do use.

Continue in this way, even as it gets more challenging, and eventually you will not have a problem with knowing whom to thank. You will begin to see the divine behind all of creation. And your complaints will become fewer every day.

Gratitude: Part II

Give thanks to those people, things, and situations in your life that seem negative to you.

Begin by bringing to mind someone close to you who is often irritating or troublesome. Imagine what your life would be like if this person suddenly disappeared—wasn't changed, wasn't less troublesome, but was completely gone. If you think you would miss the person, say an internal thank you for that presence in your life.

Now look at the petty tyrants in your past: bosses, teachers, parents, lovers, or others. Recall your reactions to them and the final outcome. You may have learned to leave a bad situation or to make the best of it by detaching from their irrationality. You may even have learned compassion for them in spite of their power over you.

If any of these are true, thank that person for what your interaction has taught you.

Remember your critics: those who have flung verbal stones at you, who may even have known how to immobilize you or trigger your deepest shame. If, from any one of these, you received information that you have been able to use, internally thank that person.

Consider your enemies: people who have made it their business to get in your way, to stop you, to hurt you. How did you cope? If you became stronger in order to deal with one of them, thank that person for offering you a training ground. If under this duress you discovered compassion for one of them or for yourself, thank that person for providing the occasion for your learning.

If what you learned from any one of these people was how to leave, to get away, to protect yourself, even at the cost of embarrassment, alienation, or serious loss, thank the person who provided you with that lesson in clarity.

If in any of these cases you find it impossible to thank the person involved, then thank the universe for offering you this situation for your training.

If your memory brings you to a time and place where you received nothing except damage to yourself—where you became less in every way—admit it fully. Remind yourself that human life does include such situations. Then look for a way to give thanks anyway.

You may be able to thank your own body for surviving, or your mind or spirit for not giving in. You may be able to thank some person or circumstance that helped you make it through. Or simply be grateful that there was an end.

But also try this. Looking back at that time, say to it, "Thank you. I don't know why you happened, or for what purpose, but thank you." Without demanding that understanding come, without expecting healing, say "thank you" to the evil that once held you.

If the evil—the situation or person—is not in the past but in the present, say, "I don't know why you are in my life, but thank you for being here." Pretend it is a teacher whose ways are mysterious and say thanks with as much of your heart as you can. Don't expect to be repaid with understanding or with anything at all. Just give thanks.

If you find yourself feeling anger or outrage, notice where it lives in your body and how it feels.

Now find your way back. Take several deep breaths. Move your body, touch your skin or massage it, bringing yourself back into concrete physical sensation. Let yourself rest.

If you find yourself caught in bitterness, regret, or other difficult emotion, you may begin the meditation again. This time, work with your problematic emotion and look for a way to thank it. (Alternately, use the "Exploring Anger" meditation from part 5.)

If this meditation triggers feelings of unworthiness or shame, stop immediately and find your way back. Wait awhile before trying it again. When you do, test it cautiously. When you respond with curiosity, surprise, or even amazement, then you are ready to work with it.

Postlude

Waking up this morning, I vow with all beings to embrace everything without exception.

—ZEN MORNING VERSE

The taste of freedom leaves us forever unsatisfied. Nothing is so compelling as that. If you are not compelled by it, then know you haven't tasted it yet.

The taste of freedom leaves us forever satisfied. Something rises within, becomes alive, knows it has come home. Beyond this are layers and layers of coming home, opening after opening, until the journey itself becomes our home.

May you soon remember who you truly are. May you be happy. May you be free from suffering. May you be at peace. May you know the joy of your own true nature.

Appendix

The Hsin Hsin Ming (Trusting the Heart-Mind) was written by Seng-ts'an, known as the third Zen patriarch in China—a student of a student of Bodhidharma, who brought Zen from India.

This version is by Steve Hagen, based on several translations of the original Chinese.

The Hsin Hsin Ming

The Great Way is not difficult
for those who have no preferences.
Only when you neither love nor hate
does It appear clearly, without disguise.
A hair's breadth of difference
and heaven and earth are set apart.
If you wish to see It,
then hold no opinions either for or against.
To set what you like against what you dislike
is the disease of the mind.
Not knowing the profound quality of the Way,
we disturb our original peace of mind to no purpose.

Perfect like great space,
the Way has nothing lacking, nothing extra.
By our accepting and rejecting,
we lose sight of the true nature of things.
Neither chase after outer entanglements,
nor dwell in Emptiness.
Be serene in the oneness of things,
and confusion will vanish of its own accord.
When movement is stopped in order to get rest,
this rest will itself be restless.
If you linger in either extreme,
how can you realize that there are not two?
Without a thorough understanding of Oneness,
both movement and rest will be insufficient.
Banish reality, and you fall into it;
seek Emptiness, and you deny Its nature.
The more talking and thinking,
the farther from the Truth.
Abandon wordiness and intellection,
and there is nothing you cannot penetrate.
Return to the root, and discover the essence;
pursue illumination, and lose the source.
The moment we see within,
appearance and emptiness are transcended.
The recurring movement between apparent and empty
arises only because of our ignorance.
Do not seek after Truth,
only cease to cherish opinions.

Do not remain in the relative view of things;
avoid such pursuits carefully.
If there is the slightest trace of this and that,
the mind is lost in confusion.
The two exist because of the One,
but do not hold on to the One.
When the mind is not disturbed,
there is neither offense, nor blame.
When nothing offends,
the multitude of things vanish along with the mind.
When no discriminating thoughts arise,
the mind ceases to exist.
When mind vanishes, things follow it.
Object is object for the subject;
subject is subject for the object.
The thoroughgoing relativity of these two
is originally One Emptiness.
In Emptiness, mind and thing are indistinguishable
and each contains within itself the whole world.
If you do not discriminate between coarse and fine,
how can you be for this and against that?
The Great Way is All-embracing;
It is neither easy nor difficult.
Limited views are flighty and insecure—
now rushing headlong, now holding back.
In clinging to "this," which is beyond measure,
the mind enters a path which leads it astray.

Let things take their own course,
and experience neither going nor staying.
Obeying the nature of things, we are in accord with the Way,
wandering freely, without annoyance.
When our thought is fettered, it turns from the Truth;
it is dark, heavy, unclear.
The burdensome practice of judging
brings annoyance and weariness.
It is foolish to irritate the mind;
why shun this to be friends with that?
If you wish to enter in the One vehicle,
do not flee from the six dusts.
Indeed, not hating the world of the senses
is identical with true enlightenment.
The wise have no motives;
fools shackle themselves.
There is one Dharma, not many;
distinctions arise from foolishly clinging to this and that.
Seeking the Mind with discriminating mind—
is not this the greatest mistake?
Ignorance begets motion and rest;
Wisdom neither loves nor hates.
All dualities derive from false inference.
They are like dreams, phantoms, flowers in air.
Why so anxiously pursue them?
Gain and loss, right and wrong—
away with them once and for all!

If the eye does not sleep,
all dreaming will naturally cease.
If the mind makes no discrimination,
all things are as they are of a single essence.
In the deep mystery of this One Essence,
entanglements drop away.
When all things are seen equally,
timeless Thus-in-Itself is reached.
Forget the "why?" of things
when there can be no measuring or comparing.
When motion stops, there is no motion;
when rest is set in motion, there is no rest.
Since "two" cannot be established,
how can there be One?
Arriving where there is no further,
there can be no law or description to apply.
For the unified mind in accord with the Way,
all self-centered striving ceases.
Doubts and irresolutions vanish;
faith is confirmed.
There is nothing left behind,
nothing to remember.
Empty, lucid, self-illuminated,
the Mind does not exert itself.
This is where thought is useless,
what sense or feeling cannot fathom.
In this world of Suchness,
there is neither self nor other.

*To come directly into harmony with Truth,
all that can be said is "not two."
In this "not two," nothing is separate,
nothing is excluded.
The enlightened of all times and places
have all entered into this Truth.
This Truth is not extended in time or space;
for in It, a moment and an eon are one.
There is neither here nor there,
yet this Truth is manifest in all directions.
The infinitely small is as the infinitely great
when limits are forgotten.
The very large is as the very small
when outlines are dissolved.
Being is an aspect of non-being;
non-being, an aspect of being.
Don't waste time in doubts and arguments
which would not have It so.
The One is none other than the All;
The All is none other than the One.
If only this is realized,
the rest will follow of its own accord.
Trusting the Heartmind is the "not-two,"
for non-duality is one with Faith.
This is where words fail,
for the Way is neither yesterday, today nor tomorrow.*

Notes

The Dream Time

1. Stephanie Coontz, *The Way We Never Were: American Families and the Nostalgia Trap* (New York: Basic Books, 1992). The title tells the story of this book: it's full of statistics contradicting our most common assumptions about American life, past and present. One poignant example: today about 20 percent of American children live in poverty. But in 1900 about 20 percent of American children lived in orphanages—their parents were living, but were too poor to support them!
2. Quoted by Tenshin Reb Anderson in a lecture at Hokyoji Zen Monastery, Memorial Day sesshin, 1993.
3. Matthew 27:46 New American Bible.

Life Is Like This

4. Shunryu Suzuki, *Zen Mind, Beginner's Mind* (Boston: Weatherhill, 1983). This Zen classic is the source of this and later quotations by Suzuki.
5. From the comic strip "Calvin and Hobbes" by Bill Watterson, June 6, 1993. Used by permission.
6. Colin Turnbull, *The Mountain People* (New York: Simon and Schuster, 1972). Turnbull's two years with the Ik, and his reflections on what it means to be human as a result of meeting them, are described here.

We Want to Be Happy

7. Thomas Cleary, ed. and trans., *Timeless Spring: A Soto Zen Anthology* (Boston: Weatherhill, 1980). The conversation about the "most miserable state" is one of numerous stories of monks and Zen recorded in this book.

When You're the Other

8. This story is retold and discussed by Clarissa Pinkola Estés in *Women Who Run with the Wolves: Myths and Stories of the Wild Woman Archetype* (New York: Ballantine, 1992): pp. 164–96.
9. Archie Fire Lame Deer and Richard Erdoes, "Thunder Dreamers," in *Gift of Power: The Life and Teachings of a Lakota Medicine Man* (Santa Fe, N. Mex.: Bear & Co., 1992): pp. 162–72.
10. Maledoma Patrice Somé, *Of Water and the Spirit: Ritual, Magic, and Initiation in the Life of an African Shaman* (New York: Putnam, 1994): p. 61.

The Human Condition

11. Exodus 34:7, Authorized (King James) Version. Emphasis added.
12. Ibid, emphasis added.
13. This meditation is adapted from one by Stephen Levine in *Who Dies? An Investigation of Conscious Living and Conscious Dying* (New York: Anchor Press, 1982): p. 81–83.

Hope

14. *The Honour of All: The People of Alkali Lake*, video produced by Four Worlds Development Project for Alkali Lake Indian Band, British Columbia, 1986.

15. Romans 8:28 NAB
16. Job 1:21 AV
17. Stephen and Ondrea Levine, *Relationship as a Path of Awakening* (Chamisal, N. Mex.: Warm Rock Tapes, 1990). Audiotape.
18. This meditation is adapted from one I heard by Ram Dass in Minneapolis in 1984.

What Do You Do?
19. Genesis 32:23–32

Author's Note

Special thanks go to two people without whom this book would not have happened. The first is my life partner, Jean Captain. She encouraged me, critiqued and read and reread the manuscript innumerable times, and supported me financially during much of the writing. The second is Scott Edelstein, my literary agent and editor, who not only believed in my work from the beginning but who helped me bring it forth.

I also want to thank my other readers—Carol Huge, Jackie Captain, Kate Greenway, and Arlene Minatelli—for their insightful comments and encouragement. My editors at Tuttle—specifically Michael Kerber and Isabelle Bleecker—have been gentle with the manuscript, respectful toward me, and immensely patient.

Thanks to my parents, Martin and Virginia Huge, for support of many kinds, including financial. Thanks to my daughters, Joy and Robin Dickey, for who they are and what they have taught me, and for being in my life now as adults, by choice.

There is a conversation of sorts, which has nourished me and kept me sane, that appears here and there in this book. Thanks to the many people who have shared that conversation with me, including particularly Kate Greenway again, Denise Wilder, Rebekah Donicht, Evangeline, and the late Michael Macmacha.

Thanks to Robin Wilson, who introduced me to the healing modality that reorganized my life and who remains one of my mentors.

Thanks to the friends with whom I have exchanged healings over the years, nurturing my whole being through caring for my body and exploring new possibilities of mind and body: Sandi Weis-Freier, Lee Beaty, Martin Bulgerin, Holly Stone, and Arlene Minatelli once more.

I am deeply indebted to Reb Anderson, my Zen teacher. I hold enormous gratitude to Shohaku Okumura, the late Dainin Katagiri, and the community of Minnesota Zen Meditation Center. Though that community includes many individuals who have helped me, I am particularly grateful to these, who were like my elder sisters and brothers along the way: Joen Snyder-O'Neal, Yuko Coniff, Shoken Winecoff, Judith Ragir, Mike Port, Teijo Munnich, Dokai Georgeson, Jisho Cary Warner, Steve Hagen, Michael O'Neal.

The writing of this book was a journey in itself. I found myself saying things, again and again, that seemed insufferably arrogant—that claimed personal knowledge of ultimate truth; that told other people what to do; that seemed entirely out of place for me to say. I would put in qualifiers: "I think" or "It seems to me." My editor took them out, again and again, until finally I understood that they interfered with what I was saying and started to take them out myself.

The result is a kind of breathlessness about this work. In many ways I don't even know where it came from. I must know it, for I wrote it, yet I am astonished. Sometimes, during the last year of writing, I would turn to these pages looking for help with my own life. Sometimes I found it. Sometimes I saw the inadequacy of my words and rewrote, looking for my own answers. Sometimes I was unable; sometimes even in writing I could not reach the place where I knew. But overall, it taught me.

So my last thanks are to the work, to the writing itself, which became my teacher.

Some Favorite Books

These books (and those above) have moved me, taught me, changed me, inspired me, or helped me. They work with the spirit in a wide range of ways.

Sacred Stories, Fiction, Essays, and Memoirs

Allen, Paula Gunn. *Grandmothers of the Light: A Medicine Woman's Sourcebook.* Boston: Beacon Press, 1991.

Allende, Isabel. *Of Love and Shadows.* New York: Knopf, 1987.

———. *The Infinite Plan: A Novel.* New York: HarperCollins, 1993.

Cameron, Anne. *Daughters of Copper Woman.* Vancouver: Press Gang Publishers, 1981.

Eliach, Yaffa, ed. *Hasidic Tales of the Holocaust.* New York: Oxford University Press, 1982.

Goldberg, Natalie. *Writing Down the Bones.* Boston: Shambhala, 1986.

Grahn, Judy. *Another Mother Tongue: Gay Words, Gay Worlds.* Boston: Beacon Press, 1984.

Jung, Carl. *Memories, Dreams, Reflections.* New York: Random House, 1989.

Kusz, Natalie. *Road Song: A Memoir.* New York: Farrar Straus Giroux, 1990.

Levine, Stephen, *Healing into Life and Death.* New York: Anchor Books, 1989.

Lessing, Doris. *African Laughter: Four Visits to Zimbabwe.* New York: HarperCollins, 1992.

Lorde, Audre. *The Cancer Journals.* Argyle, New York: Spinsters Ink, 1980.

Matthiessen, Peter. *Nine-headed Dragon River: Zen Journals.* Boston: Shambhala, 1985. The Narihara quotation comes from this book.

Monaghan, Patricia. *The Book of Goddesses and Heroines,* second edition. (St. Paul, Minn.: Llewellyn, 1990).

Moraga, Cherrie, and Gloria Anzaldua, eds. *This Bridge Called My Back: Writings by Radical Women of Color.* Watertown, Mass.: Persephone Press, 1981.

Mountain, Marian. *The Zen Environment: The Impact of Zen Meditation.* New York: Bantam, 1983.

Nanamoli, trans. *The Life of the Buddha As It Appears in the Pali Canon, the Oldest Authentic Record.* Ceylon: Buddhist Publication Society, 1972. Nanamoli has taken stories of Buddha's life from numerous sources and arranged them chronologically. Many passages describe enlightenment as the realization that "All that is subject to arising is subject to cessation."

Walker, Alice. *The Color Purple.* New York: Washington Square Press, 1982.

———. *In Search of Our Mothers' Gardens: Womanist Prose.* New York: Harcourt Brace Jovanovich, 1983.

———. *The Temple of My Familiar.* New York: Harcourt Brace Jovanovich, 1983.

Practical Books

Alexander, Christopher, et al. *A Pattern Language: Towns, Buildings, Construction.* New York: Oxford University Press, 1977.

———. *The Timeless Way of Building.* New York: Oxford University Press, 1979.

Colt, Lee. *Listening: How to Increase Awareness of Your Inner Guide.* Wildomar, Calif.: Las Brisas Retreat Center, 1985.

Dominguez, Joe, and Vicki Robin. *Your Money or Your Life: Transforming Your Relationship with Money and Achieving Financial Independence.* New York: Viking Penguin, 1992.

Hendrix, Harville. *Getting the Love You Want: A Guide for Couples.* New York: HarperCollins, 1990.

Sher, Barbara. *Wishcraft: How to Get What You Really Want.* New York: Ballantine Books, 1979.

Buddhism

Aitken, Robert, trans. *The Gateless Barrier: The Wu-Men Kuan (Mumonkan).* San Francisco: North Point Press, 1991.

Beck, Charlotte Joko. *Everyday Zen: Love & Work.* New York: HarperCollins, 1989.

Katagiri, Dainin. *Returning to Silence: Zen Practice in Daily Life.* Boston: Shambhala, 1988.

Suzuki, Shunryu. *Zen Mind, Beginner's Mind.* New York: Weatherhill, 1970.

Tanahashi, Kazuaki, ed. *Moon in a Dewdrop: Writings of Zen Master Dogen.* San Francisco: North Point Press, 1985.

Trungpa, Chogyam. *The Myth of Freedom and the Way of Meditation.* Boston: Shambala, 1976.

———. *Cutting through Spiritual Materialism.* Boston: Shambhala, 1973.

About the Author

Janet Cedar Spring is a practitioner of Zen and the cofounder of Ravenswood, a spiritually-oriented retreat center in northwestern Wisconsin. Currently Cedar lives with her partner in Duluth, Minnesota, where she writes, teaches, and works as a psychotherapist and holistic healer. For information about Ravenswood write to:

Ravenswood
P.O. Box 1131
Superior, WI 54880